LOOK! I WILL HELP YOU

LOOK!
I WILL HELP YOU
YOU

LOOKING AT LIFE WITH NEW EYES

POST-PANDEMIC

Sarah Gillon

Matador
Unit E2 Airfield Business Park,
Harrison Road, Market Harborough,
Leicestershire. LE16 7UL
Tel: 0116 2792299
Email: books@troubador.co.uk
Web: www.troubador.co.uk/matador
Twitter: @matadorbooks

ISBN 978 1803131 245

British Library Cataloguing in Publication Data.
A catalogue record for this book is available from the British Library.

Printed and bound in Great Britain by 4edge Limited
Typeset in 11pt Minion Pro by Troubador Publishing Ltd, Leicester, UK

Matador is an imprint of Troubador Publishing Ltd

This book is dedicated to everyone who reads it.

CONTENTS

ACKNOWLEDGEMENTS

To the love of my life Jon for always believing in me and encouraging me in everything I decide to do in life.

For my three beautiful children Amy, Mason and Scarlett who inspire me every day.

To my wonderful mother and father for your help and guidance, and my brother and family for their support over the years.

To Uncle Frank and my grandparents who I miss every day. To my mother-in-law Val and father-in-law John who continue to be an inspiration to me.

To everyone, too many to mention, who have been a massive influence in my life, and to all my family and friends, I love you and thank you all.

INTRODUCTION

I have written this book so that I can try to help everyone who reads it and hopefully they will pass it on to their families so that they can read it too. I would like to help as many people as I can so that they can learn to live a more stress-free life. I would also like everyone to find that peace within each of them.

I always see the beauty around me in nature and in everyone I meet. I also try to treat everyone how I want to be treated. I am relaxed and don't seem to worry about all the little things that pile up. I am never deeply depressed, though I of course will have a sad day, moan or get frustrated. I have the same feelings that come and go like everyone else. The difference is that I notice that this lasts only for a short period of time, a moment, an hour or a day or two at the most. Everyone else I see depressed for weeks, months and even years. I don't suffer as much because I believe it is the way I look at life. This is what I have written about and passed on to you in this book. I believe that if you try to do as I do, you will feel lighter and will start to feel peace within you. Living your life each day a lot more content and happier. This is how I feel, and I pass on everything that I know to you all – I hope it helps you.

I believe that you can do this, just like I have. So, let us begin this new way of looking at your life, beginning with chapter one.

ONE

BE OPEN-MINDED

LOOK AT WHO YOU ARE

This is going to be hard for you to do, I mean, so hard. Can you truthfully, I will say that again, *truthfully* look at who you are?

It is so hard to acknowledge our faults. Basically, we always make excuses for our behaviour or blame someone else for who we are and what we do.

"If you didn't do that then I would not have done that to you" or "if I wasn't running late, I would not have…" or "if you didn't say that to me, I wouldn't say that about you".

See how easy it is to talk and take the blame away from what we have done and from who we are. No one else in that moment said or did something. We did it, and we were the ones who said it. Sometimes it is hard to look at ourselves, and we don't like to admit we could be tired, angry or maybe worried. These and so many more emotions can be so strange and hard to cope with. We just lash out and act out on them to make us feel better. Sometimes we do this when sad, hurt and frustrated – we need to face who we really are, to just say "*yes*, I am in the wrong" or "I do need to improve myself in a certain area of my life". Maybe you need to be aware that you can be selfish only wanting things your way and not thinking of anyone else around you.

So really look at every aspect of yourself. Little steps will always make a difference. Try to be aware of what you are doing, saying and how you act all the time. Admit it and embrace that life is hard. Everyone is trying their best, no one is better than anyone else. All it is, is the choices we make to where we are today. *Free will* is there for all of us to put to good use. I realise that we are all born into different families and circumstances which can have a profound effect on us all, and this will make a difference in how we see things. We are all just trying to find our way in this life. We walk along, side by side, in different styles but ultimately the same direction, until it is time to leave this earth. Please remember to look at how you are walking the path next to your fellow man/woman. Are you true to yourself? Are you open to change for the better? Are you willing to try? And I mean try hard, as life is hard and you need to work on yourself. Always try to say the right things so that you do not say mean things to make yourself feel better, because that is what you are doing; instead, say kind things to someone to make yourself feel better. Don't just say "I can't be bothered" or "it's too much hassle" or "it's too hard" or "I haven't got time". Maybe you think they will not notice or that they don't care anyway. They will notice and they do care even if they do not show it. Take that time to do something that will make a difference. Even if you do not see the results. The results will be there, so be bothered and change for the better. Then watch the ripple effects that follow. One day, you will see or hear the difference you made; sometimes it will not show straight away – it takes time. Change will come for the better; it will appear. Try *now* – try to improve; try to be better; try to make a difference somehow. Try in any area you choose. Work hard on it and then sit back and await the results.

You will feel so proud of yourself.

THINKING ABOUT YOURSELF – POSITIVE AND NEGATIVE

You can look at this subheading in two different ways.

First way:
Thinking about yourself is important. You are a very important person; you are wonderful and have something special and unique to give to the world that will help to make it a little bit better because *you're* in it. Here, now and present, this moment, this second, you. If you do not think you have anything to give to the world, you are a hundred per cent wrong because you are a hundred per cent important. Only you are you – remember that we all have special qualities about each of us. Someone could be amazing at taking photographs or drawing and this makes people happy when they look at the pictures. You could be amazing at making people laugh. This makes people's hearts feel lighter and happier. Someone could be a

good listener; this makes people able to share ideas or feelings with them.

Thinking about yourself is important in different ways. It is also needed so that you look after yourself properly with food, rest and love. We all need these things for ourselves so that we stay healthy and strong.

Thinking about yourself and your circumstances could be important so that you make that difference in your life to change a negative into a positive.

If you are around people who are not helping you to develop in a more positive way, then maybe you should think about moving forward without them. If you are in a relationship which is not good for you, for example. You will know if the friendship or relationship is not right for you because you will feel uneasy, worried, scared and uncomfortable. These are not normal feelings, and you should never feel like this when you are in the right relationship and friendships.

Only be around people in your life who you can relate to and be a hundred per cent yourself with.

- *You are amazing* – say this out loud.
- *I am amazing.*
- Say it louder.
- *I am amazing.*
- Yes, you are.

So *never* forget it and be the *best* you can be in all aspects of your life. Please make sure you think kindly of yourself and treat yourself with the love and respect *you deserve.*

Second way:

Next, you could say thinking about yourself could be a bad thing as this is selfish and self-consuming. This can make you not see what's in front of you. You could miss other people's feelings as you're caught up in yourself so much. Now, I want you to know that thinking about other people can be such a fantastic thing to do; you feel so good in helping people. You should try; it will take your mind off your worries as then you are not thinking about what is upsetting you in your life – not thinking about that will be a breath of fresh air. Concentrating on someone else will lift you up; even if you do not understand why, you will feel so much better for doing it. Thinking about yourself can also be a negative thing in that it can emotionally drain you and even make you feel depressed, all because you're focused on yourself. So, sometimes when you focus on yourself and think about you and how you are doing, it is a good idea to try and balance it out with thinking about others as well. That way, you look after yourself because you are an amazing person, and you can think about other people at the same time. This will help to make you feel good in a different way; you won't overthink everything and then life will just flow a lot easier. Have a look at yourself and give yourself a pat on the back.

Remember that you're unique and a wonderful person.

CHANGE IS CONSTANT

Be open for change always taking place because it will always be happening. Time goes by, and hours, days, months pass. The seasons of life go by where every age you become feels different. You are always changing: your face, body, height; a boy's voice box deepens; children's feet will grow. Everything is growing, even your feelings, emotions and ideas change all the time. Places where you grew up look different. A house may have been painted a new shade of colour. A tree could have been cut down and a new business may have opened its doors. It just does not look the same anymore. You yourself also may have moved home lots of different times or moved jobs. You may decide tomorrow to go and get your hair cut or want to pop in to visit a friend. I could go on and on as so many things change all the time.

If change is always constant, the best thing we can do is always move forward positively. Do not hold onto the past but enjoy the memories until new, fresh memories are made in the future. Through this constant change, always learn new things and skills. Also, begin to be aware of who you are and what your positive potential is in life, improving yourself through all you do. Use change to explore the world around you. Look at change in a positive way and enjoy the new opportunities it brings forward in your life.

BAD DAYS WILL COME AND GO; GOOD DAYS WILL COME AND GO

Always remember you will get bad days in your life every week, month and year. You are not alone as every single person on this planet will also get bad days in their lives too. You will have days you are feeling down, depressed or something will happen to upset you and even make you cry or feel terrible. Just remember, life is going to be like that, and unfortunately, you may seem to have a run of months, and even years, with more bad days than good. Remember it's half and half usually; if you have a few years of seemingly bad days all together, then you are due to have a few years of good days too. The old saying is that you cannot have the good without the bad because you would not understand or appreciate the good days unless you experience the sad ones too. The main thing to realise is that every day is a fresh start; you can reside in the bad day or try to rise above it and change it into a good day. Sometimes you cannot change circumstances, and you may find it hard to change how you feel because it's just too painful, but please remember time will make it into a good day again. Nothing stays the same as everything is constantly changing. Look forward to the good days that will a hundred per cent come along. Look forward to moving up and beyond the bad days. Keep saying to yourself that this state you're in will not last; nothing stays the same. You can even say this out loud if it helps to keep this message clear in your mind. Change will inevitably happen.

Remember that the future will be better.

LIVE EVERY MOMENT IN THE MOMENT

Live every moment in the moment; this way, you will never have any regrets. The moment has passed and gone, so why look back unless it's for happy memories? The past has helped to mould you into who you are today. Not everything, but a lot of circumstances can affect each of us differently during our life. Do you like who you are now, in this moment in time? If you like you, then that's great, but if you don't like who you are, then now is the best time and the best opportunity to live how you have always wanted. In this moment, it is about becoming a new and positive you. Guess what, the past has gone. The now is present; the future has not been moulded yet. Do not worry – this can last forever. What I mean is if every moment is fresh and new, then this is your time to shine and be who you want to be. You can do this by taking this new way of looking at each moment to break any bad habits you have or by just starting afresh. By using positive feelings, positive thoughts and positive actions in this moment in time. The more you practise this, the better and easier it will become. Then you will enjoy being in this state and live automatically in every moment. Looking around you with fresh eyes and looking for the positive that is just waiting to be found. This new outlook will then bring forth a knock-on effect of positive thoughts, positive action and then positive changes in your life. Have a go – *see what positive things happen to the new you.*

REVIEW

Let us go over what has been written in Chapter One – Be Open-Minded.

Look at Who You Are
Try to improve and work on yourself. Be open to change, make that difference to your life and to others around you.

Thinking about Yourself – Positive and Negative
Look after yourself – you are amazing (remember that always). Do not be self-absorbed think about others too.

Change Is Constant
Be willing to accept change and enjoy it, using the new opportunities to your advantage.

Bad Days Will Come and Go; Good Days Will Come and Go
Never forget good days will always come along. The bad days will fade away.

Live Every Moment in the Moment
Every moment is a fresh start and an opportunity to make things better. Also, enjoy each moment by being present and aware of everything around you and what you say and do.

FOCUSING ON CHAPTER ONE – BE OPEN-MINDED

Please say the following statements out loud to help you. Repeat them as many times as you like. Whenever you need some extra support. I will also write statements after each chapter that follows for you to say out loud as well.

- *I will make a positive difference in my life. I will look at who I am and how I can improve myself.*
- *I am amazing.*
- *I am fabulous.*
- *I am beautiful/handsome.*
- *I am the best.*
- *I am wonderful.*
- *I am unique.*
- *I am open to change. I will not let the past hold me back.*
- *I will start today to make new and positive memories.*
- *Today is a fresh new start. I will do the best I can. I will live in the moment and only focus on the now.*
- *I will practise positive thoughts, positive feelings and positive actions from this moment and every moment onwards.*
- *This state I am in will not last – nothing stays the same. My future will be brighter.*
- *I will be patient and then change will happen in my life.*

I am love.

TWO

POSITIVE ONE

NICE THOUGHTS; NICE THINGS

We all like things in our life, and we all enjoy thinking nice thoughts and doing nice things. So, what nice thoughts do you have? What things do you like to do? Maybe something from your childhood that makes you feel warm and remember the love and comfort you received. Maybe a memory makes you feel young again and brings back happy childhood experiences, or you may like to watch a cartoon. I love to watch *Toy Story*, *Sponge Bob*, *Mr Bean* and *The Polar Express*.

You could look at old photos and videos that will put a smile on your face. Painting a picture or making something can be relaxing. You could buy a magazine or read a new book. How about painting your nails and toenails, trimming your beard or getting a different style haircut? You could go out and have a go at bowling or visit a museum. Buy that toy you always wanted as a child. You could go to the park and feed the ducks. Eat your favourite food and really think about how much you enjoy it.

Also, do nice things for other people in your life and say nice things to make them feel good. You will then feel great too from doing this.

Find some paper and write a list of things to do straight away which are affordable and manageable and will make you feel nice. Then, every week, pick one off the list. You can then just keep on repeating the list, or you could make a new one every month or year.

Next, you could write letters to everyone saying nice things to them. If you don't want to give it to them straight away, hold onto it until the right moment presents itself. Maybe a birthday or a special achievement in their life. You could even write a letter to yourself about all the nice things about you.

You could decide to go and buy a pet. Pets are great to make you feel nice. Petting them and playing with them is very comforting. There are so many different pets to choose from. I have had lots of different pets over the years. They have all been lovely and brought me hours of nice memories and happiness.

So, make sure to do nice things in your life to make you feel better. Anything that doesn't hurt anyone that makes you feel happy is great.

POSITIVE ATTRACTS POSITIVE

Like attracts like; positive attracts positive. Which would also mean that negative attracts negative. This tells us that maybe we need to change our negative thinking into positive thoughts and then action, which will then attract positiveness towards us.

Do you find a lot of negative things seem to pop up in your life? Let's try to get the positive things into your life instead. Let's have a go and see if it works.

If you walk into a room, you can sometimes sense the positive or negative. You can feel the emotion in the atmosphere, which means it will most certainly affect you.

If it's a negative atmosphere, you don't want to feel uncomfortable so you would of course keep clear of that section of the room. This would be the same around a particular person – someone could send out nice and positive energy which you feel comfortable to be around or dark, negative energy. Which, then, do you choose to be around?

Of course, if you are choosing positive then you will get on better with everyone around you. You can do this just by changing the negative attitude of thinking the worst about everything. Instead, try to be positive and look at the good things. Keep optimistic and imagine a positive and good outcome with whatever you do or say. Always remember that a smile, a happy attitude and bright outlook on life will make the world of difference. People love being around that positive atmosphere, *and they will love being around you too.*

Think of positive sentences to say out loud which will help to make you feel better and optimistic about your life.

- *I am happy. I am content.*
- *I will feel good today.*
- *I am great.*
- *Yes, I can do it.*
- *I am so proud of myself.*
- *I can make a difference, and I will make a difference today.*
- *I am strong and full of love.*
- *I feel positive, I am positive and everything I do will be positive.*

Open your eyes and be proud of yourself. Also, open your heart and make room in your heart.

Be here and be present; stop looking to the past unless it's to remember lovely memories. Don't look towards the future too much but just enough for positive thinking and to look forward to the future with fresh, positive ideas. Be positive in the here and now as today will make the difference for tomorrow. Now is the time to make that difference. Even little steps will all help. Remember that doing little things will always snowball into bigger steps and bigger things.

Don't worry about the amount of time either; anything positive is worth it. Just try not to let time slip by with nothing done. Unless, of course, you're still for a reason (rest, meditation or watching something). Just remember that if you're aware of all you think, say and do, you will then make a difference in the world. All through thinking and acting positively.

LOOK TO THE CHILDREN

We have all heard of the saying "to be childlike". Well, what this basically means is looking at how children communicate and look at the world. They do this differently than adults. We become harder and not as sensitive sometimes as we grow older over time. Children, on the other hand, are still fresh and innocent and do not carry the baggage of life. We should try to follow children's example and look at their different qualities and put them to good use in our own lives.

We should not judge each other. Children accept what you say and do not question your honesty because they themselves are honest and just say what they think. Children look up to adults for advice and guidance. Maybe we should start to look up to each other as well. Children enjoy life and love to play together or just have fun playing on their own. We also need to have fun in our lives, whichever way we go. Children do not plan ahead as much as we adults do. Children just live for each moment of time; we need to try our hardest to do the same. Children love people and especially animals. They also have a lot of energy and are inquisitive and love to know how everything works and why it's the way it is.

If we could look at all the different things that make children the way they are and how they look at life, we would learn so much from them. Try to add some new aspects I have mentioned into your own life.

INNOCENCE

What did you want to do when you were young and still that child – can you remember what it was? Have you achieved what you wanted or imagined? Are you happy? Or did you not end up where you imagined or planned to be?

Look back and remember who you were when you were a young child. Get back to that part of you that is still there if you look underneath the everyday things of life that can weigh us down or load on top of us. We are still those children we used to be. We just need to find the child within each of us and get some innocence back. See things in our lives from a different, fresh perspective. Look through our eyes from that child's point of view.

What do you see? Are you happy? Are you content? What would you keep?

This child within you can find the right path, especially for you. So be that child for a moment and review your life up to the present moment. What will you keep? What will you change? What do you need?

Let's make it happen.

TOGETHER STRENGTH

Try not to isolate yourself, and let people around you into your life so that you are not on your own all the time. The company of others is so good! Being connected feels great, talking about your life and listening to others talk about their lives. This is what will help you to develop as a person. Talk to your friends, acquaintances and family. This can be a great way to have fresh ideas and inspiration to move forward with your life. Maybe finding the encouragement that you need to start a fresh project you have had in mind or bring forth a new idea into your life. Sometimes by working with someone, this will give you strength and confidence to make so many things happen. Which, if doing on your own, maybe you would feel unsure of. Working as a team and this collective feeling of belonging is great. When you are all working towards the same goal.

We also can feel lonely when on our own. So, of course, it is lovely to have the company of others in our life. To share love and give strength and confidence to each other. To be happy, we need to communicate with each other and enjoy each other's company.

Life is all about sharing and bringing the best of each other out in the open. Please encourage everyone you meet to be the best they can be and encourage yourself to do the same.

FIND THE GOODNESS

Look around you – what I mean is look closely at what goes on. You will find goodness around you in your everyday life. People helping each other, people friendly, happy and smiling, you will notice that people want to get on with each other.

Sometimes life is hard it's a struggle and people are not concentrating on what's around them or their minds are not present – they are away sorting out problems and issues that need looking at.

If you concentrate on what is positive around you, this will then bring forth hope, comfort, happiness and contentment. Finding all the good around you will encourage you to try harder in your own life. Remember that focusing on the positive is so much more productive than having a negative outlook. So, always try to look for the good in all situations presented to you and with all the new and familiar people in your life.

Of course, if your instincts tell you to stay away from a situation or a person then that is completely different; you should then listen to what your heart tells you. Maybe someone you first meet makes you feel uncomfortable and uneasy when you are with them. Always listen to your instincts and stay away.

In all other situations, remember to look for the good in all you see, do and who you meet. Life will start to look a lot brighter if you do that.

REVIEW

Let us go over what has been written in Chapter Two – Positive One.

Nice Thoughts; Nice Things
Remember to do what feels nice and makes you feel happy. Also, try to think nice thoughts – this will have a knock-on effect.

Positive Attracts Positive
Please try to think positively and then act positively. This will help you so much.

Look To the Children
We need to find our inner child and look at the world around us with a new, fresh perspective.

Innocence
Let us find our innocence again. This will help us to find and then sort out what is needed in our lives.

Together Strength
Not being alone is important – share your journey with others and help each other to be the best that we can all be.

Find the Goodness
Look and find the good in all you see and who you meet. This will help to highlight all the amazing things and people around us.

FOCUSING ON CHAPTER TWO – POSITIVE ONE

STATEMENTS TO SAY OUT LOUD:

- *I will do nice things in my life to make myself feel happy.*
- *I will say nice things to everyone in my life to make them happy.*
- *I am nice.*
- *I am lovely.*
- *I am kind.*
- *I am thoughtful.*
- *I am brave.*
- *I will look at life through a child's eyes.*
- *I will be more childlike.*
- *I will not struggle on my own. I will ask for advice and help when I need it.*
- *I will find the good in everyone.*
- *I will find the good in me.*

To get rid of negative feelings, repeat and say in order as follows:

1. *I release all negative thoughts.*
2. *I release all negativity that is stuck on me and in me.*
3. *I am now free of any negative emotions.*
4. *I am going to embrace only positive emotions.*
5. *I am positive – I am going to only think positive thoughts.*
6. *I am going to only do positive actions.*
7. *Positivity is my new compass. I am full of positivity.*

I am love.

THREE

POSITIVE TWO

MIND OVER MATTER

The way we all look at life, everyday situations and decisions can have a very big effect on us. Mind over matter means that how we look at these things in life will decide how we feel. If we look at things with a negative view, then we will be only sad, angry, nervous, depressed and all the different negative emotions. We really don't want that, so instead, we need to think only of the best in every situation. That way, we will feel stronger in all these everyday situations.

If you are, for example, nervous about going to the doctors, then by the time you're in the surgery, you will be in such a state that whatever happens will seem so much worse. On the other hand, if you had gone to the doctors in a positive frame of mind, when you were in there you would be relaxed and at ease over the situations presented. These two different aspects of how you look at something in life can make an enormous difference to how you will feel and deal with everyday things that occur.

When I look at the older generation and see men and women who live a productive and healthy life into their eighties and nineties, they all seem to have one or more things in common. That is being active and having a positive outlook on life. They are all strong minded and have a "let's carry on" type of attitude. This is what we all need to do too.

I really believe that stress and thinking negatively, only seeing failure, can have a major effect on the body. If you suffer with your health, please try to blank out any negativity which you are dwelling on. Look at the chapter on meditation which could help you to relax. Also, try the meditation exercises I recommend. If you put your mind to it, you can do it. *You can do anything.*

MAKE THE BEST OF WHAT YOU HAVE GOT

I have heard of this saying before, "to make the best of what you've got". This is a good and solid piece of advice and makes complete sense. There is so much to be thankful for. You have family, a home, food, care, comfort and love. If you don't feel that you have a lot of these things, you still have some of them. It's a fact that when you look back at the past, life could be a lot harder in so many ways. Here are but a few:

no washing machine, no television, no car, no duvet cover, no phone. I could carry on and on depending on when in history we look at. Also, some people in the world don't have the basic things we take for granted. We need to realise how precious life is. Look at your work colleagues, friends, family and appreciate how they are there for you.

We are all trying the best we can. Enjoy your life; embrace all of it. You don't want to keep desiring more and wanting more. That will not make you happy in the long run. A second of happiness will fade away; you want constant happiness and to get that you will need to look at life differently. This is one of those things you need to realise, that if you are so busy trying to get more and more things, you will miss out on everything around you.

Also, there is always someone worse off than you. So, really look at what you have; really look at your friends and work colleagues; even look at all the people who you meet every day. Maybe other parents at school or your local newsagent staff. Maybe your postman/woman. Appreciate all and everyone in your life. If your family is poor, still appreciate all you do have. You can always improve your situation. Just make sure you smile while you are doing it. Don't moan or doing that will bring your mood down and everyones around you. As I mentioned before, the way you think and then act has a knock-on effect. Please remember that positive thinking and being content will make a big difference to everyone around you and *especially to you*.

CONFIDENCE TO LIVE LIFE TO THE FULLEST

Please have confidence *now*, not when you're older. Now is the time to try to do what you want in life. Everyone I have spoken to who is a lot older always says, "if only I knew then what I know now and I had all this confidence when I was younger".

So, please try to move out of your comfort zone a little and then you can shine.

Speak about your thoughts, feelings, ideas. People will benefit from your input in life. Speak to people one on one and then get involved where your point of view can be heard. Voice your ideas and opinions – you could make a big difference in someone's life. Remember that everyone is just like you and me. They also have family, houses and they need to pluck or shave hairs, blow their nose and do all the same things in life like we do. So, please believe in yourself as we are all equal beings. The confidence you have in life can benefit so many people. Depending on what you use your confidence for. Use it for something good, something to help people. We all have something unique and individual that is only in each one of us. No one else has the same as we do – whatever this is should be shared and given to the world. So, what is your unique gift?

Maybe you're good at maths or catching a ball. Maybe you're good at doing make-up or maybe you're great at smiling and brighten up everyone's day.

Whatever it is, you will have something great to give. So, beam with confidence and give what only you can, the best unique ability from you. If you haven't figured out what your gift is, ask friends and family what they think you're good at. Ask what your strengths are in their eyes. Also, don't worry if you still don't know. Time will open it up to you, maybe next week or month. Maybe even years into the future. One day, you will realise what your strength is and then you can use it.

You own confidence – *show the world how confident you can be.*

CHOICES/FREE WILL – WHAT AN AMAZING GIFT

Free will is such a huge statement. It means you can do whatever you want in this world. The possibilities available to you are endless. Now, really think about that!

Life is there for everyone to choose to do the right thing or to do the hardest, and sometimes even the wrong thing. It's all up to you because if you have free will then every second of every day you can choose any word or sentence to utter. You can go left, right or jump up and down. You have an infinite number of options you get to choose between, and this ultimately means you can do whatever you want in life so long as it is within the law.

You choose your job, friends, clothes, food, entertainment, living arrangements, partner, and you even choose your whole life. So, please don't moan or have a go at anybody about your own free will and the choices you have made in life. You and only you can change anything you want to make it a better life.

You could decide to join a new course so that you can get out and meet new people. Maybe you decide to paint your kitchen yellow to brighten it up. You could decide to slow down and just stay at home a bit more with the family.

This is all your choice – please make the right choices for you. Also, remember that all your choices and free will can and will affect everyone around you. Choose wisely, kindly and take the right path for you. Always with *love* at the front of your decision-making. Then you will never go wrong.

YOU ARE NEVER ALONE

Remember that there are always other people in the same position as you who may feel alone. At some point, or even times of each day, we can all feel lonely. Find people who feel the same and talk to them. Friendship is a great thing, even if only to text or chat on the phone. Maybe a course would help – new people are at new courses. You could meet someone this way.

If you don't want to talk to people, you can always talk to animals. Even better, just buy a new pet or adopt one. Then at least you will always have someone who will listen to you and keep you company.

You could even talk to nature, the trees, flowers, wind, sun or moon. Try to connect and you will start to feel better. Remember that people love to interact with each other. Find people who share your interests. See what local events are on in your area. Even go and say hello to your neighbour. They may feel the same as you and want someone to talk to. Maybe you could set up your own group to meet new people.

There are so many people outside your front door – go for a walk and connect with who you meet. While out, say hello and reach out to them, talk about your life and ask them about theirs. Sharing is great; you don't feel alone and then you won't be alone. Get in contact with an aunt, uncle, brother or even a great aunt or uncle. They may like the company and would love to have a chat. You may think of someone else from the family to visit. Remember that you're never alone and there will always be people who you can talk to.

REVIEW

Let us go over what has been written in Chapter Three – Positive Two.

Mind over Matter
You can do anything if you put your mind to it. Think positively and stay focused – go towards your dreams.

Make the Best of What You Have Got
Love your life; appreciate what you have. Look at your family and friends and realise how lucky you are.

Confidence to Live Life to the Fullest
Share and live with confidence to develop into the best person you can be.

Choices/Free Will – What an Amazing Gift
Make good choices in life. Choose using love as your guide.

You Are Never Alone
Reach out to people. Connect, talk and share. You will find that people want to help you.

FOCUSING ON CHAPTER THREE – POSITIVE TWO

STATEMENTS TO SAY OUT LOUD:

- *I can do anything I put my mind to.*
- *I will succeed.*
- *I am brave.*
- *I am happy and content with who I am.*
- *I am full of confidence.*
- *I choose love as my guide.*
- *I am never on my own; people are all around me. I will connect with who I meet.*
- *I love being me.*
- *I am free to be me.*
- *I am free to choose who I want to be.*
- *I choose to be the best version of me.*
- *I am only going to pick things in my life which will help me become the best me that I can be.*
- *From this moment on, I am going to become who I am supposed to be. The best of who I can be and that is me.*

I am love.

FOUR

THE SERIOUS ISSUES PART ONE

SUFFERING MENTALLY AND PHYSICALLY

There is so much suffering in the world, physically and mentally. Life is so hard to deal with.

Everyone says we can all cope with what is thrown at us from life. Suffering in any form can be the hardest blow of all. Which can make us crumble. So, how do we cope with suffering?

Suffering mentally can be painful, lonely, draining of energy, unbearable and so many more feelings.

Physical suffering affects the body and mind. Draining your energy just like mental suffering. The pain can be unbelievable, unbearable and even make you feel in shock or depressed. We can only deal with it the best way we can, until it goes away. Nothing will ever stay the same. We know that suffering will eventually disappear, however long or short that will be.

Mental suffering needs lots of understanding and support from people around you. Professional, qualified people can also help. You may need to change your whole way of thinking or do something new and fresh to break through your mental struggle. It may be a long time before the pain passes or eases.

Try to talk to people who care about you. They will give their utmost to make sure you feel better in any way that they can to help you.

Physical suffering can sometimes improve with help from doctors and professional specialists, medication and even operations. Unfortunately, you may lose the use of some part of your body. Please try to think about all the other positive bits of your body you can still use. If you can use your whole body, then please appreciate it all as we should realise how lucky we all are. We really should take a moment to focus on what wonderful bodies we have. You may be suffering from an illness that leaves you exhausted. Try to keep up as much positivity as you can through this difficult time. Just do whatever small things you can every day to break up the routine. This will help to keep you motivated.

The same is helpful with mental suffering – doing something every day to keep your mind occupied will also take your thoughts away from yourself. Which will ultimately help you.

Time is a big key to any suffering, and time will help ease any pain. In the moment of suffering, you will not see anything positive. Please believe me when I say that you are never alone. Someone will be there for you; be strong and hold on until it passes away. You can and will get through any suffering. Believe in yourself and let others help you through this part of your journey and this uncertain period of your life that you are suffering.

Everything will be OK, be patient, you can do it.

I believe in you.

ARGUMENTS

Arguing will just weigh you down; you will feel so tired from all the energy you have used up. It is such a waste of energy. You could use that energy in a positive way and not on someone who is not being nice to you. Or maybe you were the one to have a go at someone. So, before you do argue, see if you can sit down and discuss all the details of why you or the other person is upset. Arguing will just make all involved angrier and your blood pressure will rise. This will not make you feel any better, just worse. Things could even escalate to a higher level of arguing, so calming down and not answering back is always best. It can be so hard not to answer back when you are in the middle of an argument. I myself have been guilty of doing just that. I can't seem to help myself. So, if, like me, that happens to you, just start afresh from after you have answered back.

Instead, calmly say, "if you are not going to say anything nice or positive, then don't talk to me".

Then carry on calmly with your day away from that

person. If they follow you, then say, "excuse me" and then move into another room.

If they still follow you, just go outside or go to the local shop. Just put some distance between you both. Then it will all calm down. Later in the day, you can always discuss things, quietly and clearly. Putting both sides across without arguing.

Unless you realise it was not worth the argument in the first place. Sometimes words can be wasted in arguments. Remember, arguing will wear you out physically, mentally and even spiritually. So, try not to bite back when someone says hurtful things, and try not to start an argument. Think about if what you say will hurt someone's feelings or make them angry. Try to discuss what you want in a more sensitive way.

Deep breathing can help when in an argument. Deep breaths do work, so keep breathing slowly and focus only on this until you calm down enough to walk away or change the subject.

There is always a better way to get rid of emotion than to argue. Maybe you could sing at the top of your lungs or ride a bike around the block. Do something that will use up that energy in a positive way.

Remember that nothing good comes out of arguing. All you need to do is calm down and then discuss things quietly.

ANGER

If you have a problem with losing your temper all the time, especially if it is over tiny issues, please think about how that is affecting everyone around you. Anger makes everyone feel miserable, sad, depressed and angry themselves. It will drain you of energy, leaving you feeling tired.

I understand that it can be so hard to control but control we must. It is the same principle as arguing.

1. Think before you lose control. Is it worth shouting about and losing your temper over or not?
2. What are you going to shout about? Does it seem a silly thing to scream over? If so, then just step back.
3. Say nothing and walk away, then keep busy and think about something else.
4. Take your mind away from what is bothering you, then, once you calm down, it probably will not seem as bad as you first thought.

If you really have a feeling that you need to scream or shout then use a pillow to scream into; at least that way you are releasing all that stored up energy that needs to come out. I would like to suggest this as a last resort though and instead, if you can, just think about how this will affect you. You will end up feeling low and upset and everyone around you will be upset too. (Is it not better to just let it all go?)

I would suggest writing everything down that is upsetting you. Then, at the end of the day, you can have a look at what is important and what is not. That way, you can discuss calmly what is bothering you without shouting and screaming to get your point across.

Anger is such a waste of your time – say this to yourself when you feel the stirrings of emotion creep up on you.

Remember that arguing and anger use up energy. Instead, put it to better use. Turn it on its head and make someone smile or laugh instead – stop it in its track. Anger will not make you happy, only sad.

Ignore your anger, take a deep breath and move forward. *I know you can do it.*

WORRY

Please do not worry about what people think about you. You are perfect just the way you are. Believe in yourself and look at your strengths. Focus on all the positive things you do. Remember that most people are insecure about something, either the way they look or what they do or say. Always find greatness in yourself and others, then you will not worry as much. You will just live each day as it comes. Which is what each of us should be doing, living in the moment. Do not worry about every little thing. Sometimes it is not your responsibility, you may take everything off your shoulders. It feels great to just let it all go or let someone else take over for you. Drop it for a moment, take a break, breathe and relax.

If you are worried about something, write it down. Then you will not keep thinking about it all the time. Lists are great – stick lists inside or on your kitchen cupboards. I do this, then you will have reminders of what needs doing or what decisions you need to make. It really does help a lot to stop the worry.

Things sometimes seem so overwhelming, and you just want to stop worrying. You can stop the worrying and, even better, you will. Just write it all down and empty your mind. If you do this then maybe an hour, a day or a week later, you will either have a great idea to help you or your worry will not seem so big to you. Something may happen to stop the worry, just wait and see. Worry will always come and go, you just help it to go away a lot sooner.

Remember that worry is just a moment in time – *it will pass.*

GUILT

We have all done things we regret in life. You are not on your own in this. I'm sure everyone on the whole planet has done something or said something hurtful more than once. Probably a lot of times when they look back on their life so far. Everyone will wince, get embarrassed, feel sad or upset about what has happened or because of what's been said. In the moment, we all do and say things which a split second later we wish we hadn't done as that is imprinted on our life forever, or is it?

What I mean is, there is a way to make yourself and whoever you upset feel better if you feel guilty over anything in your life.

Just do it; just say sorry.

It may seem so hard to do, but it is only a second of uncomfortableness. Once you have said it, you'll feel rejuvenated, fresh, free, strong and so, so good. If you really find this task too unbearable to do, then please consider instead writing a letter, and make sure they receive it. On the end of the letter, leave your phone number, address or email. They may ring or write back to you. If they do not reply, at least you tried. That would be great. If it is too late to say sorry as you don't know where the person is or if someone has passed away, you can still say sorry to them. Say it out loud as if they were in front of you. Maybe do it when you are on your own. Say what you would like to say if they were listening.

Please read the sentence below when and if you say sorry to someone:

You should be so proud of yourself. You should stand tall and proud. I say to you, well done, you did it. Notice how light and relieved you feel. A weight has been lifted off you that you have carried around; this is a new start for you. Always, from now on, be aware of what you say and do to the people around you. Treat them how you want to be treated and you can't go wrong.

REVIEW

Let us go over what has been written in Chapter Four – The Serious Issues – Part One.

Suffering Mentally and Physically
Let time heal you, and let everyone in your life help you.

Arguments
Slander and argue with no one. If someone is not nice, warn them once; warn them twice. Then have nothing to do with them.

Anger

Anger is such a waste of time and energy. Make someone laugh instead.

Worry

Worry will come and go. Help it to disappear, write it all down and think how wonderful you are.

Guilt

Say sorry – you can do it. Then you will feel fabulous.

FOCUSING ON CHAPTER FOUR – THE SERIOUS ISSUES – PART ONE

STATEMENTS TO SAY OUT LOUD:

- *I am not alone – I will get through this time in life.*
- *I will strive to find positive things in my life to focus on.*
- *I will open my heart to receive love, care and understanding from all and everybody I meet and know.*
- *I am strong and I am going to get better, physically and mentally.*
- *I will feel whole again – I smile and feel my heart fill up with hope, faith and love.*
- *I will be strong; I am strong.*
- *Strong is here to stay.*
- *I am going to feel better.*
- *I am feeling better.*
- *Every day I will get better and better, bit by bit.*

- *I am strong, brave and full of love.*
- *I will not argue – instead, I will talk quietly or say nothing at all.*
- *Arguing is a waste of my energy.*
- *Anger is a waste of time.*
- *I don't need anger anymore.*
- *I will respect my body.*
- *I will not worry anymore. I am letting go of any worries I hold.*
- *I have no worries.*
- *I am going to say sorry to anyone I have hurt in my life.*
- *I am sorry.*
- *I am strong.*
- *I can do it.*
- *I believe in myself.*

I am love.

FIVE

THE SERIOUS ISSUES
PART TWO

DON'T WANDER AIMLESSLY

Sometimes you find that you go round and round in circles. Life can end up being just about waking up, eating, working, eating and sleeping. Instead, life should be so much more. Do not wander aimlessly – find that purpose in life. When you think that it is all over, please, please try again. Do not ever give up; do not run round in circles. It is sometimes good to have a plan and not just stay in the same routine because it feels safe.

If you do want to stay in the same routine – I myself like a routine – then please try to do different things in-between that routine. Maybe you could take up a new hobby or make some new friends, think of new ideas or something new to help someone, a new holiday, a new day trip, a new job. Try to change your routine. Then you will experience new things, new people, and this will make everything feel more alive. You will then notice more around you.

Sometimes we all take things for granted. Then we stop noticing, so have another look right now. What do you see? Your family, your home, your food, your bed, your games and phone, bed covers, clothes, bath/shower, shall I go on? We are all so spoilt – look around you – we all have these things that we have and need. We live in a modern world. Where l live, I have luxury after luxury. I am not living in a poor country. I have so much more than I will ever need. Do I appreciate it all?

Do you appreciate it all?

Most of us do not even think about it; we expect it all to be just so. As everyone says, living during this day and age, we are a throwaway society, which can blind us to life – we just carry on in this easy life we live. Not really trying our hardest and not bringing out the best in each of us to share with each other. So please really think about how lucky you are. You have so much – now look again.

Now, do you see?

You are like a king or a queen; you are a king or queen of your own life. You can live like any king and queen and do whatever you want. So, use your power wisely and do what is right to make your kingdom happy, healthy and help make it thrive and grow. Producing happy, content, hard-working people. Kings and queens want the best for their people.

Bring peace to your castle. By first seeing all before you, good and bad. Plan well, with lots of new ideas and objectives to strive towards. Also, make sure it is done in a positive way so that only an abundance of happiness, love and peace will be produced, and then move forward and prosper. Now go forth and rule your kingdom in *love*.

FORGIVENESS

Forgiveness is a really big thing that everyone can really struggle with. I am sure we all have someone in our lives who we just cannot forgive. They hurt you, wronged you. Maybe they made you feel sad. Someone may have physically hurt you or someone you love. It is difficult to understand the way people think. They can hurt you so easily and sometimes do not realise that they even have.

It could be because they are having a hard day and just took it out on you. Maybe it was a deliberate dig or action at your expense. There are so many reasons why we just cannot forgive.

Unfortunately, this is something we should all be really trying to do. It is so important for our very own well-being to be able to forgive that person/people in your life or those who you do not even see anymore. It does not matter if it is even someone who has passed away. You need to try and forgive them. This will then lighten your heart. Take that weight away which is dragging you down. You may not even realise that this baggage of unforgiveness is really affecting your whole being of who you are. I know that we have all heard of this from other people, but they really are winning if you still hold onto that anger of unforgiveness. If there are a few people who you cannot forgive, then try with the person who you feel has done the least damage to you.

Now, together let us choose to get rid of that baggage of unforgiveness and let it all go.

Repeat after me:

I forgive (name of person). I let go of all the anger, sadness and stress that I am carrying connected to (name of person). I release it back into the atmosphere to disappear. I do not need to hold onto that unforgiveness any longer. Go, be gone and never return to me. Goodbye forever.

Now, take some deep breaths in and out. When you have done this, relax. Feel proud of yourself; feel happy. You have released yourself from so much anger, stress, tension and sadness. Tomorrow when you wake up, you will feel lighter and happier.

Maybe then you could forgive each person in your life. One by one and then day after day. If you do not feel ready to, then wait a few weeks and try again. If you still cannot do it, just keep on trying until you do, *because one day, you will.*

LIFE CRISIS

Sometimes you can let a midlife crisis or life crisis ruin all that you have made and built around you in your life. Even breaking up your family and friends, please do not do this. Instead, consider all the other options before changing your life. Make sure it is really what you want. Look at everyone around you, especially your family, and see how much you take them for granted. Try afresh with your family before making any rash decisions. Remember and look at all the positive things in your life. Look at what you love in this life. A lot of people have a midlife crisis around forty/fifty years old. Please do not let this age or any age get you down. As you know, there are always going to be people who are older than you. When you think about this, it can make you feel a little better. Everyone will be the same age one day. Also, it is true that with age, really does come some advantages.

1. Confidence – we always get confidence the older we get and the more life experience we have.
2. Life experience – you cannot beat living for thirty, forty, fifty, sixty, seventy, eighty, ninety or more years for life experience so that you feel settled in the world.
3. Scared – nothing is as scary because you have mostly dealt with a lot of your childhood fears.
4. Knowing what to do – you know and understand how to do most things, like cooking, washing, bills, car maintenance. If you have children, then you've gained a whole variety of skills.
5. Appreciate more – you appreciate things more as you get older.
6. Worry – you worry a little less about the little things, like you do when you are younger. Also, you do not worry as much what people think.
7. Understanding people – you understand people a little bit more. It takes this long to figure out why

people are the way they are. This will make you more relaxed around people too.

I am sure there are more things I have missed out. I hope you can see from this that being older is a positive thing. Embrace it, enjoy it and learn from it. You have so much experience and knowledge to pass on to the younger generation.

Be proud, stand tall and share your story.

DON'T GIVE UP

Sometimes life is hard and can make you feel depressed and fed up. You need to hold on to that one thing that makes you feel alright. Alright is good – it is something to work on. Just find that nice thing in life and concentrate on it. Maybe a friend or relative, a place, an object, a memory. Whatever feels positive then just keep meditating on it so that you feel the positive vibes and they stay around you a bit longer. Then if it is possible, see the person; find the object. Think about making some new positive memories, maybe in a different way.

How you look at things in your life makes such a big difference. Positive is positive thinking and negative is negative thinking. Everyone does seem to attract whatever way they think. So, if you are upset or down, you can sometimes seem to have a run of things always going wrong for you. If you think positively, then you can sometimes seem to attract positive feedback from all round.

Find someone to talk to – this will help to sort out your feelings and emotions. Making a positive plan that you can follow would be great. Hearing someone else's perception of your life and what they would suggest may help. As everyone sees things differently, they may think of something which you would never have dreamt of. This new bit of advice from someone could change everything.

Making small, positive changes in our lives can lead to lots of other positive things happening. Change can be great for growth and then it can lead to other fresh ideas forming.

Reach out to people – do not be shy, awkward or embarrassed. Everyone has hard times or feels low. People just do not talk about it or are not good at sharing their feelings and showing their vulnerable side. Most people put on a brave face. If only we all knew their drama in life, loneliness, their heartache. We would be surprised how many people have so many different difficulties in some aspect of their life to deal with.

Just ask advice from a neighbour, a friend, a family member or even someone you pass every day when you go walking. Maybe you could speak to the people who work at your local store. People who you always say hello to and meet regularly. All you need to do is find a phone number or email address from using Google. There are so many organisations that you will be able to talk to and places to visit – the main thing is not to give up.

It is not just yourself you have to think about. It is the people who love you – how will your sorrow affect them? They could become depressed or berate themselves over what they should, and could, have done differently to help you more. The knock-on effect of what you do is so much bigger than you will ever realise. Always think about how what you do could affect family, friends and colleagues as you are connected to everyone who loves you. They may be struggling themselves and you could help each other together.

Remember that you are never alone; you are loved; you are alive. Strive to make life happier.

Think about this famous saying: "behind every cloud is a silver lining". This means that you should never feel so low as to feel like you want to give up because difficult times are like the dark clouds that block out the sun. The clouds will always move away and part so that the sun can shine again. Which would mean that better days ahead are coming. The sun will always come out again, given patience and time.

Remember that life is beautiful, so keep moving forward. Step by step, day by day and week by week.

You can do it – I believe in you.

DON'T JUDGE OTHERS OR BE JEALOUS OR ENVIOUS

Please do not judge others or be jealous or envious in this life. Why would you be?

Everyone has great things about them, from looking amazing, to their body being amazing, to being amazing at different sports, to being clever at activities like making clothes, drawing, science, gardening, driving, inventing, calculations, DIY or caring for others. We are all amazing in some way.

If someone has a good job or has a lot of spare money to buy whatever they want, please do not be envious of this.

Instead, you should be happy and just agree that they are fortunate. Sometimes having money and being able to buy things is not going to make you constantly happy as it is a fleeting contentment, and the only happiness that lasts is not from having money. Inner happiness comes from being happy and content in all of life's situations, not just from material things and what money can buy. So, do not judge people or feel jealous or envious of what they do or have. Remember that they may not be as happy as you think; you may be surprised to find that you would not want to be in their shoes. So, in that case, jealousy and envy is a waste of your energy and will just weigh you down and make you feel unhappy or angry.

Instead, cut away these emotions and feel light and free. Focus on all the positive things in your life and work towards other positivity to help make you feel proud and happy.

You do not need jealously or envy in your life. Rise above these emotions and just be happy with who you are and where you are.

REVIEW

Let us go over what has been written in Chapter Five – The Serious Issues – Part Two.

Don't Wander Aimlessly
Find your path and give it your all. Make life amazing and help as many people as you can.

Forgiveness
Try to forgive all who have wronged you. You will then feel so much lighter and so much happier.

Life Crisis
Turn it into positivity – you now have confidence, life experience and know what to do in different situations presented. You also appreciate more, understand more, do not worry as much and are not as scared. So, please use all these gifts you have to your advantage.

Don't Give Up
Keep moving forward, little by little and step by step. You can do it – follow the light and it will shine brighter every day. Patience will help, and believing in yourself. You can do it – I believe in you.

Don't Judge Others or Be Jealous or Envious
Jealousy and envy are a waste of your energy. Don't judge others; instead, concentrate on thankfulness for what you have, and look forward to your own positive future and start making happy memories.

FOCUSING ON CHAPTER FIVE – THE SERIOUS ISSUES – PART TWO

STATEMENTS TO SAY OUT LOUD:

- *I will make a positive difference in my life.*
- *I will make a positive difference in someone else's life.*
- *I will forgive whoever hurt me.*
- *I forgive you.*
- *I forgive myself.*
- *I love me; I love being me; I am love.*
- *I will be the best that I can be.*
- *I am happy; I am content.*
- *I will feel good.*
- *I am great.*
- *Yes, I can do it.*
- *I will not give up.*
- *I am so proud of myself.*
- *I can make a difference, and I will make a difference.*
- *I love myself, and I love everyone – I love all.*
- *I will not be envious.*
- *I will not be jealous.*
- *I will not judge anyone.*
- *Jealousy and envy are a waste of my energy.*
- *I will be happy for other people I know.*
- *I am thankful for what I have in my life.*
- *I am happy to be me.*
- *I am kind, happy and content.*

I am love.

SIX

LIFE'S STUMBLING BLOCKS

ALCOHOL, DRUGS – NO, NO, NO

Please, please, please do not rely on drink, drugs or cigarettes.

In my teenage years, I smoked heavily to help my confidence. It really was one of the hardest things to give up. I know how addictive these poisons can be. Drink can completely change the way you think.

Do you change for the better?

No, of course not, it is just a downwards spiral of anger, depression and wanting more and more and then having no money. Just living for it day by day. Sometimes you drink or take drugs to live in a dream world or for confidence. Sometimes you want to get away from it all.

There is a better way than this – any type of alcohol, drugs or cigarettes will be the worst thing to get addicted to. You will have to rethink everything in your life and dig so deep for your inner strength to get through giving up the addiction.

Once you are clear-headed and not reliant on any of it, this will be one of the best things you have done. You will feel so proud of yourself and of what you have achieved. Also, you will feel fresh, brand-new, clean, alert and full of possibilities for the future. You will be able to look at life with new, clear eyes.

Life when on alcohol, drugs and cigarettes is confusing, bleary and unfocused, a struggle, frustrating and always, and when I say always, I mean forever, wanting more and more and more.

Now, if you are free of that, you will feel so much lighter. You will find yourself smiling as you are free from the struggle of addiction.

So, now you need to give up your addiction.

I will give you some advice on some things I did myself when giving up smoking. Below is a list for you to have a look at and then have a go.

1. Mind over matter.
2. Determination.
3. A goal.
4. An end treat.
5. Take your mind away with things to do.
6. Write lots of lists to tick off.
7. Buy lots of motivational books and films to watch.
8. See or talk to a professional who can help you.
9. Support from your family, friends, work colleagues.

10. A hundred per cent give it your all.
11. Think of the positive outcome.
12. Meditation.
13. Exercise.
14. Shopping.
15. Helping others.
16. Being creative.
17. Keep your hands busy – writing, drawing, painting.

Remember that addiction can take over your life. Your choice, your family and your desire for more and forever more. Now you will take over that addiction by stopping it. You will have all the power instead – enjoy being in control and not letting the addiction rule you and your life. It will not be easy to do, it will be hard work, but I know you can do it. Just like I gave up cigarettes, for good! *You can do it too.* I believe in you – come on, let us not just try but let us be free from addiction, starting now.

Hello, freedom.

TOO MUCH INFORMATION; TOO MUCH TO DO

There seems to be too much information in life. Everywhere you look, someone is telling you what to do or giving you lots of information. Usually, you find this out from your phone, tablet, computer, television and adverts on your phone and TV, emails and your local paper. It is all around you, this can make it hard for you to think for yourself and use clear thoughts free of clutter in your mind. I know it can be hard to cut back. I would even consider going as far as not to use any phone, tablet, laptop or television for two whole days straight. Obviously do this when you have no work commitments. Then see how you feel. I bet you will be a little lost as we all rely on all the information that we look at everyday in our lives. It is part of most people's daily routine. Once you get used to the silence and so much more time available, you will start to wonder what to do with yourself.

Now is the time to do all the things you have been putting off, or you can come up with new things you may want to have a go at. The ideas will keep flowing when you stop everything and quietly decide on an action plan, try it and see for yourself.

There is too much to do every day in life. Shopping, bills, school runs, car maintenance, tidying, rubbish, hoovering, meals, looking after your family, the list goes on and on. This can all be so tiring and wears us all out.

Make time for your family – we should always make time for the people we love. Do not say, "I just need to do this or that". You will never have any time free unless you make the time available.

We need to decide to have one whole day doing nothing. Let everything go for that one day and do nothing. Do not cook; just have a sandwich and fruit. The less done on this day the better. Completely relax or do something for you instead. Maybe you could paint a picture or write a poem. You should not do anything to do with life's chores. This will then help you to have a restful day and maybe a creative day instead. You will hopefully feel refreshed, energised and a lot happier the next day when you get up. If for some reason you do not, then I would suggest doing a couple of extra days again. You obviously need a lot of rest to feel better.

Try it and see.

CAN'T DO IT? PLEASE TRY, AND TRY AGAIN

If you feel fed up because you cannot seem to do what you try so hard to fulfil, just keep trying and do not give up because you can do it, and you will do it. Sometimes you just need more practice, and then some more practice, before you can achieve what you want to do.

Most people, when asked how they succeeded in whatever they have done, will say, "I just kept trying, and I didn't give up".

Sometimes it takes a lot of time and effort. Have a look back on all the things you gave up trying to do. Why not have another go at them and this time you may surprise yourself? Determination and a positive outlook will always be a great way to help keep you going. You can and will succeed. Please just remember to keep trying and carry on with that positive attitude every step of the way.

If you do what I suggest but still cannot succeed at what you want to achieve, take a rest and know that you really tried your hardest. Feel proud and stand tall, knowing that you did all you could. It is time for a new goal. Let us think about a new project or achievement we would like to start or have a go at. With all of this in mind, just go for it with the same enthusiasm, determination and positivity as before.

There will always be situations and things in life we do not want to do or even think about. Maybe going to the dentist or the doctors. This can be a big challenge for all of us. Things like this are so important; you should always attend even if you feel scared or nervous. Facing things early will work out better in the long run, before your symptoms develop and more worries and pain occur.

If you are worried in life, please try to face up to your fears with little steps at a time. This will be better than doing nothing. Ask for professional help if it is a big issue that affects your life.

Do not let fear ruin all the opportunities in life that are waiting just for you.

Anything you feel like you cannot do, please remember to just try. At least have a go and really look at the situation and realise that it is not as hopeless as you may think. You can do it, and you can do anything. So, try your best; that is all you can do.

Keep trying.

PATIENCE, PATIENCE, PATIENCE

Patience can be so hard to hold onto. Especially when certain situations arise and seem to irritate, aggravate and upset you.

If you try your hardest, patience can be the key to lots of situations being resolved or stopped in their tracks. Patience is great because it helps to stop things from getting out of hand when you are in the middle of an argument. You just need to decide not to join in the conversation; instead, you wait quietly until the person has stopped talking. If you do not reply to someone then there is no argument to have. So, patience is amazing when you look at it from that point of view. Also, if you have patience then you will not say the wrong thing in the spur of the moment. It will also mean that you will not make a wrong decision without really thinking about it.

Remember earlier in chapter one when I talked about everything being constant change. Well, this moment will also pass. If you were to use patience, it would help the situation presented to resolve itself a lot quicker.

Patience should be used for all negative situations and emotions you face in your everyday life. If put to good use, you will notice the difference and will feel more in control, calm and empowered by doing the correct action in any situation presented. Patience is amazing when used and will help in so many scenarios.

Practise using your patience more and more. Then put it to good use and enjoy watching the results.

REVIEW

Let us go over what has been written in Chapter Six – Life's Stumbling Blocks.

Alcohol, Drugs – no, no, no
Let's have a clear head, positive, energised body and spirit in full control and ready for a bright future without addiction.

Too Much Information; Too Much to Do
Have a rest from all the chaos; have a day free of all electrical appliances. Enjoy being able to create, fix and fulfil all the ideas that you have imagined.

Can't Do It? Please Try, and Try Again
You can do it; give it your all. You can always pick another goal to work towards. Keep trying and stay positive.

Patience, Patience, Patience
Patience is great – always use it to make any situation better.

FOCUSING ON CHAPTER SIX – LIFE'S STUMBLING BLOCKS

STATEMENTS TO SAY OUT LOUD:

- *I don't need any addiction in my life.*
- *I am free of addiction.*
- *I will never be addicted to (insert substance here) again.*
- *I will create new ideas and then new positive things in my life.*
- *I will make time to do all the things in life that make me smile.*
- *I will keep trying until I succeed.*
- *I will have patience in all negative situations that I find myself in.*
- *I am free.*
- *I am full of creativity.*
- *I have unlimited patience.*
- *I will keep smiling.*
- *I am happy.*

I am love.

SEVEN

SIMILARITIES AND DIFFERENCES

EVERYONE THINKS DIFFERENTLY BECAUSE EVERYONE IS DIFFERENT

Everyone is unique, completely, utterly unique. There is only one of you. So, it stands to reason that we would all think slightly differently. No one else is inside us. We all have completely different experiences in life. For example, we may have different childhoods, happy, sad, caring or uncaring parents. This will affect our personalities and how we view life.

Every second of every day shapes us all the time into who we are, in that moment and every moment after that.

We could all be standing in the same situation and

every single one of us would do something slightly or dramatically different to each other. Also, depending on your temperament – calm, laid-back people will of course cope better than nervous, angry or agitated people. This all makes a difference to how we act in any given situation.

You should always remember that everyone thinks differently which means that everyone sees things differently.

Let us have a look at an example. Let us say that you sent someone a message on your phone: "I fell over when I was out with Beth today".

Someone could see this text and say to themselves, *Beth probably pushed her or, if she didn't, why didn't Beth stop her from falling over? Beth isn't a good friend.* When in fact, Beth was buying you both a drink at the time and was nowhere near you when you fell over.

So, people either do not know all the information and decide things without knowing all the facts, or people don't phrase texts correctly. In this instance, you left out important information that should have been mentioned.

Texting can be very damaging as something can just be innocently said and then, unfortunately, people misread it. Now, if you talk to someone, you can always tell in their voice if what they say is intended positively or not. The tone of your voice can be very important to express how you feel, soft and kind or loud and violent. A text message does not tell you that. Remember that you could both read the same text completely differently. If you get upset about one line of a text message, it is a very small thing to focus on when, as I have mentioned, maybe the person did not mean the message in the way you read it. Just ring them up and talk to them.

I notice that sometimes so many little things become big issues which really are not important.

If someone keeps on saying horrible things to you or puts you down all the time, that is different, and you should not be near that person. No one should be made to feel insignificant. Everyone is important; each of us can make a difference to each other's lives. The small comments, texts and attitude from people, you should just let that all go. If not, it will weigh you down, without you even knowing it.

Have a go and feel it fall away from you. The lightness will follow, and you will feel much better in yourself. Also, do not worry about what people think as long as you are happy, and you know that you're doing the right thing (not hurting anyone) and making the right decision for you.

As I mentioned earlier, everyone does think differently. Use this knowledge to your advantage. Ask people their opinion on things you are unsure of. This can give you a new perspective on things. Also, learn from the people around you. Maybe you keep doing something wrong. If you watch or ask someone how they do it differently, this could be such a big help to you.

The differences in each of us can be such a positive thing to learn and share and see different points of view.

Embrace everything different about you.

PEOPLE PUT ON A BRAVE FACE

Be aware that family, friends, colleagues and strangers sometimes do not show how they are really feeling. They could be suffering in silence, and you would never know by just looking at them. Some people, even family members, are not as open as others and can really struggle in life.

Try to be sensitive and aware of how you treat everyone; do not be harsh. What you say could affect them in a profound way. Try to say nice and encouraging things to everyone in your life or to those people you may only meet briefly. Just like you would like people to treat you gently. Just remember that we are all just trying the best we can. Some people cope better than others. We all have strengths and weaknesses in ourselves and our lives.

I may love dogs, but my neighbour is petrified of them. I could be so scared of talking in front of a group of people, but my friend may find that it doesn't bother them in the slightest. We are all nervous about different things in life, be it emotionally or physically. Many people will not ask for help, especially the elderly who do not want to be a burden or nuisance to anyone. A lot of elderly people are lonely and only see their children once a week, which is not enough if you live alone. They would never dream of saying anything to their children. We need to realise these things about family members, friends and acquaintances. Then we can help and try to make a difference in people's lives. We can offer to listen or help in any way we can. Then the people around us will not have to put on a brave face as they will be having the extra support that they need from us or professional people that we can get in contact with to also help.

Please look around you at the people in your life. Ask them how they are; notice how they act. Offer your support and be available to help. Also, if you feel like you need the support or help, just go and ask until you get the support you need.

WE ALL WANT TO BE LOVED

Please listen within to that heart of yours. All of your decisions in life should be made in love from your heart. If your heart tells you yes, do it. If your heart tells you no, then do not do it. I would find another way. It is the same as what is right and wrong – you should listen to your heart for the right answer.

The whole world and everyone in it – babies, toddlers, children, adolescents, young adults and mature adults – all want and yearn for the same thing, that is to be loved. Everyone craves love, and if you do not feel love, it can affect everything in your life. You look for it everywhere without even knowing it. Love from your teacher in the way of praise or an encouraging word in your ear. Love between friends; you want them to stay being your friend so that you feel that connection between you both which is in fact love. The love towards your grandparents or even love between you and your pets.

Love is all around us, we just need to search for it, find it and keep working at keeping it. Lots will depend on how we treat the people around us. Whether we treat people correctly with kindness, understanding, care, encouragement and finally, love. You will then notice and feel that love being given back. Even if only in a small way. Little gestures can always build up into more love. So, to be loved you will have to give love.

Love will always solve every problem in this life. You just need to use it. Loving someone will also calm a situation down. Love will always bring a smile to someone's face and give warmth on a cold day. Love will do wonders, so let us use it in everyday life and in all situations presented. See with your own eyes the ripple effects of love extend out to the people around you. They will then carry that love and pass it on to who they meet up with. Give as much love as you can and make everyone's day better. Love is the answer, so give your love to all. It is free and the best gift you can give anyone.

Love, love and more *love.*

WE ALL FEEL THE SAME

We are all universally the same – all of us all over the world and on this planet are made up the same and of the same material. We all have bodies with skin, hair, bones, cells etc. We all have feelings, good and negative. We all laugh, cry and can get hurt. We all need to eat, drink and use the bathroom every day. We also need to sleep every night. Please remember that we are all made the same, which means that we are all equal. The differences are life experiences and our own strength and weaknesses. If you realise this fact of us all being equal, it will make getting along with all the variety of personalities that people have so much easier.

We really are all the same. Also in the way we begin life and then in the way we all grow from childhood through to adulthood and then pass on at the end of our lives. The differences being the age that we pass on, life experiences and our feelings when facing each new situation that we encounter.

Life can be joyful, and it also can be difficult – it all depends on how you look at life and deal with the situations that come up. Our daily struggle to survive is the same. Try to treat each situation with love and not fear. Love will make life easier and everything in general better.

As we are the same, then show love to everyone you meet. With a kind word or gesture.

Love is the answer; *love* is the key; *love* is free.

REVIEW

Let us go over what has been written in Chapter Seven – Similarities and Differences.

Everyone Thinks Differently Because Everyone Is Different.
Use the differences between you in a positive way. Learn and teach each other to live a better life.

People Put On a Brave Face
Try to be aware of everyone around you in your life. Do they need help? Just ask them and give what help you can, then find others who can help as well. Always ask for help for yourself when you need it.

We All Want to Be Loved
Everyone needs love, so spread that love. The world and your

own world will be better and a happier place. All you need to do is love everyone you meet. With a smile, a kind word and gesture.

We All Feel the Same
Realise that we all need to do the same things: eat, sleep and brush our teeth. Our daily struggle to survive is the same. This realisation will make meeting people and all situations in life easier. So, be positive and don't forget that love is free.

FOCUSING ON CHAPTER SEVEN – SIMILARITIES AND DIFFERENCES

STATEMENTS TO SAY OUT LOUD:

- *I am proud of myself.*
- *I will help whoever needs my support.*
- *I will be sensitive to other people's feelings.*
- *I will listen to my inner voice and only work in the power of love.*
- *Love will be my focus and guide in life.*
- *I love to love.*
- *I love my body.*
- *I love myself.*
- *I love you.*
- *I choose love.*
- *Love is free.*

I am love.

EIGHT

TO HELP YOU
PART ONE

BE CREATIVE

Being creative is good to expand your imagination and also to get things out of you which have been locked away. Sometimes you can't shift the frustration, anger, loneliness, sadness, jealously, fear and all these different emotions. Why not channel them into something creative. You could do lots of different things like painting, drawing or colouring in a poster. Cut out pictures from magazines to make a collage. This will be really satisfying if you choose a topic or pictures that you enjoy or love to look at. Maybe flowers, guitars, fashion, animals, cats, colours, books, films, sayings, shapes or even clouds. The list could go on and on. You could do some other creative things like make your own birthday cards or make models. Buy some Lego sets and make them up – I've done this myself with my son and it's so satisfying. I think I enjoyed it more than him. You could make paper dolls or a paper dolls' house. You can buy so many different craft sets and projects from shops and online – planes, trains, shops, bridges and flowers are but a few. How about making some jewellery? And jigsaws are creative – once you start, it is great to keep going until you complete the picture. This is one of those creative projects that you wouldn't dream of doing but when you do, you will enjoy making it. You could even design and make your own jigsaw. Learn to knit (I love to do this). Learn to sew and then make your own pillowcase or a piece of clothing. Design something completely new, write a poem, design and make your own board game. Paint by numbers, basically do anything creative. You could even have a go at building your own shed if you want a large project to keep you busy for a few weeks or even months.

Being creative is for all ages, from children to a hundred years old and over. There is something for everyone. You just need to find what you want to do and then have a go, and you'll feel great.

Do not just sit on your phone, laptop, tablet or in front of the television. Go to the shop or order online what you would like to do or find the materials you need at home.

Enjoy creating and watch the smile break out on your face.

MUSIC AND GAMES

Play games – you are never too old. Play pass the parcel for adults, Twister and "Guess Who?". Remember those games from when you were young. Dance and sing to your favourite music. Put on a play, write the script and then act it out to friends and family. Write a song and perform it, maybe choreograph a dance routine and then dance to your heart's content. If you are on your own, don't worry, just google all the games you can play by yourself. You will be surprised at what you will find to play.

You may want to order or go and have a look at all the different games before you decide what to play. You could buy some playing cards; there are so many card games you can play. Buy a book or have a look online at all the different varieties of games you can play.

Music is great to sometimes just relax, too. Why don't you try just sit still and listen – you will be surprised how much you will enjoy doing this. Listening to your favourite singer or band will make you feel happy inside and it will bring a smile to your face.

Try all the things I have mentioned; anything creative will be great. Have fun and enjoy yourself.

SORTING OUT AND CLEARING OUT

There are two sorts of sorting and clearing out: your body and mind and your home.

SORT AND CLEAR OUT YOUR BODY AND MIND:

Clearing out your body and mind is what we should all do. This is a wonderful thing to do. You just need to stop putting all that junk food and extra puddings into your body. Try to eat your three meals a day: breakfast with cereal and toast; lunch, maybe a sandwich or salad; and then you have dinner. Do not forget to add vegetables with whatever you cook, then the main thing to do is to drink lots of water. This is a fantastic way to detox. Do not eat in-between meals; always just eat your three meals a day. This is one of the main things to do when clearing out your body; that is, to not overeat.

To clear out your mind, you will need to wipe clean all those thoughts that you have stored up. Just write them down and then blank the chaos and start to think afresh. You will probably need to repeat this over and over before you succeed. It can be hard to blank out all the things that keep going round in your mind. If you just keep trying, once you do, you will feel amazing and so light with all the things that you have been thinking cleared out. Leaving you free to have new, creative and fresh ideas instead.

SORT AND CLEAR OUT YOUR HOME:

Now, let us have a big house clear-out. We shall cut away all that you do not really need. Go round every draw, cupboard and have a look at the furniture in your home. Do you use a lot of the items, clothing or pieces of furniture in your home? I think you would be surprised at how little you use. I am certain it would only be a small number of things and furniture and not everything that you have around you.

The clothes, food, personal items and furniture can really drag you down if there is too much of something – you will feel so much better living in a decluttered home.

Have a go and clear out your mind, body and then your home. Once you have, look at how fresh and vibrant you feel as your home will look neat and so much larger than before. Your mind will be clear and your body fresh and full of energy. Try to make this a regular routine every month or so.

FOOD AND EXERCISE

You may think it makes no difference to how you feel but it really does. If you are filling yourself up on sweets, chips, fried food, ice cream, cake – and not doing any exercise – you will feel full up, stretched and then become clogged up. Yes, I love my puddings too. I find it so hard not to have three puddings in a row. So, I have written down a few ideas that I have used myself, and I hope they will help you too.

1. After your lunch or dinner, do not have a pudding. Just have a cup of tea, coffee, water or milk to wash away the taste of the food.
2. Weigh yourself every week. This will encourage and inspire you to keep up the good work. Then you can see the results of cutting out junk food.

3. Find recipes to cook healthy food. It will taste better when you have made it from scratch and cooked it yourself.

4. Cut out all the junk food like chips, fried food, chocolate, sweets. Then, you will not have any taste of it in your mouth to begin with.

The food we eat can really affect our health. We will become overweight, lazy and have no energy from eating all the unhealthy foods. If you change your diet for just two weeks, you should be able to notice the difference. You will feel fitter, more flexible and lighter. Now, you just need to add some exercises. To become fit, healthy and the best, physically, you can be. A mini exercise routine done every day is best if possible.

The first week, you will really hurt all over. The second week, you will start to see the results of your hard work. The third week, you will feel great and have so much more energy. You can make up your own routine or follow someone else on a video on your phone, tablet or laptop. You just follow what they say and repeat it every day. When you make up your own routine, you can do it slowly so as not to overstretch and hurt yourself. This should start off with a simple move, and then you just add new exercises so that the number rises from, say, four a day to ten or more, depending on how long or many you want to do.

Here are some exercises you could add into your routine: kicks, squats, sit-ups, jumping jacks, plank, crunches, arm circles, stretching, push-ups, lunges, bridge. You can always look up some exercises to add on. If you do not want to do an exercise routine, then you could always go on a bike ride every day. Some of the healthiest people I know just walk each day. This can be a simple but effective way to lose weight. Make sure you enjoy whatever you choose.

Getting fit will change your life for the better. Enjoy it and see how fantastic and fabulous you feel and then look.

So, let's get to it.

REVIEW

Let us go over what has been written in Chapter Eight – To Help You – Part One.

Be Creative
This is a fantastic way to release all that pent-up energy. Enjoy all the creativity and watch yourself smile, as it is so much fun.

Music and Games
Music will lighten up your spirit. Sing, dance and have fun playing games.

Sorting Out and Clearing Out
Clear and sort out your mind, body and home. You'll feel so much better, fresh, vibrant and so much lighter.

Food and Exercise
Changing your diet and doing some exercise will help you to feel fabulous and also to look fabulous. So, let us start today.

FOCUSING ON CHAPTER EIGHT – TO HELP YOU – PART ONE

STATEMENTS TO SAY OUT LOUD:

- *I will create something today.*
- *I will think of fresh ideas today.*
- *I will sing and dance today.*
- *I will have fun.*
- *I clear my mind of all negative emotion.*
- *I will drink lots of water to clear out my system.*
- *I will not eat junk food anymore.*
- *I will eat healthy.*
- *I feel great.*
- *I feel vibrant and fresh.*
- *I am great.*
- *I will keep up the good work.*
- *I give myself a round of applause.*
- *I give myself a pat on the back.*
- *I can do it.*
- *I am proud of myself.*

I am love.

NINE

TO HELP YOU
PART TWO

BE OUT IN NATURE

Nature can – and will, if you let it – regenerate you. Look at the beauty all around you. Most people are just so busy with life, rushing around in their cars or busy doing errands, they don't even notice or glance at what or who is around them. If you really open your eyes and look, you will see all the different wonders of life in everything and everyone around you. Nature is a special thing and is perfect to admire.

Here are some of the wonders I have thought of:

1. The sunbeams shining down through the clouds.
2. The different colours in the sky. Of course, also the sunrise and sunsets.

3. Fluffy clouds, which we all can make pictures and characters out of. Maybe a dinosaur, a chair or a hat.
4. The sound of the birds singing or watching the birds flying in the sky.
5. The beauty of every flower, tree and shrub.
6. Listening to the wind, rain or thunder can be soothing or exhilarating.
7. Feeling the sunbeams on your face.
8. Watching the sunlight reflect on the water and looking at the sunlight through the branches of a tree.
9. The grass and trees swaying in the wind.
10. Appreciating the fresh air and the gentle breeze.
11. A beach and the tumbling, crashing waves.
12. Animals, insects and all the different minibeasts.

Everything is so beautiful; being in nature could really help to relax you, being aware of all the nature around you and then admiring it all.

Find a country path to walk, maybe a brisk walk is for you. This will help make you feel energised if done with enthusiasm. You could have a slow walk so that you can admire everything you see.

You may feel like touching the grass and feeling the texture of the bark of a tree. Feel the petal of a flower, appreciate the beauty up close. Lift your face up towards the sun. Enjoy nature, that is what it is for, to be admired. You will then feel happy and more content.

Don't forget the healing power of nature.

FIND YOURSELF IN EVERYONE YOU MEET

In life if you can look at everyone that you meet as a part of you and imagine that you also are a part of them. This will always make it feel so much easier when talking to every new person you meet. Sometimes you may need that extra confidence in life, when in certain situations. Using this technique will also help. It can sometimes be hard to get along with people who you disagree with, but by seeing yourself in them, you will be kinder, sweeter and generally nicer to everyone that you meet. Remember that no one has got to be the same as you. You just imagine different parts that are like you. Maybe the outgoing part, the chatterbox part or advice part of you. You will also start to treat everyone a lot better as you do not want to hurt or upset yourself, and that is what you would be doing if you were not nice to them. If someone is sad, you will have much more sympathy for them as you will think about that sadness in yourself. You will welcome giving them some support and a listening ear. This will really help them towards taking the pain away.

Remember that if you want to treat yourself better, then treat others better too. Let us start now, and put this into practice with everyone that we meet.

LOOKING INWARDS TO FIND PEACE

Look inwards to find your peace; peace is a stillness. Peace is just a state of being. You need to find peace within and not outwards; you need to be still to find it and connect within. Slow down from that busy lifestyle that you live and stop to think about where you are and what you are doing in this moment in time. Sometimes you need to look hard and stop everything to notice that peace within, which will be waiting for you to find. Once you do, it will settle within you so that when the chaos is all around, everything will seem less stressful as you can now focus within to find that peace. Peace is gentle, soft, relaxing, content, still and at ease. Keep looking, and when you find it, you will know straight away as you will feel the peace and it will stay with you. Trying a couple of things will really help. I would suggest meditation, which we will be looking at next. Also, certain exercises, especially yoga. This is great to do before you try to sit and centre yourself using meditation. By using this technique, you could find that peace within you. Please try your best and remember that it may take lots of times or even a couple of months of regular practice before you find what you are doing it for. So many people recommend meditation to change a person's life for the better.

Give it a go; you can do it – let us start today.

MEDITATION

Meditation is used all over the world. This routine is a simple matter of stilling all those rushing thoughts that fill up your mind. Once you clear this out of the way, you can then just sit still. This will then be the perfect time for wonderful things to happen. You can also find that peace within that I talked about in the pages before. Everyone who meditates will recommend that you do this. You will have to keep a regular routine every day or every other day and practise sitting still and not moving or thinking of anything. This will be really hard to do at first, but just keep trying and it will get easier and then, finally, you will be able to do it for longer and then even longer periods of time.

BASIC MEDITATION ROUTINE:

1. For basic meditation, you need to sit down on the floor comfortably. If you need a cushion or a chair then, of course, use one as you need to feel completely relaxed.
2. Close your eyes and breathe normally.
3. Now, focus your attention on your breath. Listen and watch your breathing. In and out, in and out. Keep on focusing on this.
4. Keep doing this for as long as you can manage.

Remember to not think of anything and just clear your mind. Only focus on your breathing. There are also other ways you can meditate.

I imagine light filling my body or you can imagine light filling up family and friends' bodies. This can be a positive, great and rewarding thing to practise and to then do. Like any exercise, you need to make time to do any sort of meditation. Five or ten minutes out of each day to start with and then building up to twenty or thirty minutes. Maybe you could do a small meditation, morning and evening. Then, if you want to make it last longer, you can. Having a routine that suits you and then making that last longer could work better for you because then you could add all sorts of extra visionary imagination exercises. The two main ways of doing meditation that I use and recommend are as follows:

FIRST MEDITATION WAY:

Sit still, comfortably and straight; close your eyes. Blank all thoughts from your head. Now, imagine white, pure light filling all and every aspect of your body. Going through the top of your head and making its way down to your feet. When your body is completely full up and brimming with light, you know you have imagined enough. Now, either say out loud or in your mind, "cleanse my body; I bathe any aches and pains away with the light. All negativity in my body, mind and soul dissolve as the light washes it all away. What is left behind in me is well-being, strength, vitality and joy". Now, I want you to imagine peace flowing over you and around you and through you. Now, take five deep breaths through your nose and out again through your mouth. If you want to do this again, do as many as you want to. When you have finished, open your eyes and smile. You can make any aspect of this meditation as long or short as you want. See if you can keep the smile nearby all day.

SECOND MEDITATION WAY:

Again, sit still, comfortably and straight. Close your eyes; blank all thoughts from your head. Now, imagine the white, pure light coming into you again and filling every part of your body. Once the light has filled you up from the tip of your head down to your toes, go through all the different parts of your body one by one. Say out loud or in your mind with conviction, "my hands are full of light; they are beautiful, happy and work perfectly, thank you". Then you can move onto the next part of your body. "My back is full of light; it is beautiful, happy and works perfectly, thank you".

Keep saying this about every single part of your body. You can think of your eyes, heart, ribs, nerves, bones, jaw, teeth, tongue, stomach, nails, head, back, shoulder, neck, groin, lungs, liver, skin. There are so many other parts that you can mention. Also focus on and say any parts of your body that are struggling to work properly. This could be your eyesight that is not very good and so start off by saying what we have gone through earlier: "my eyes are full of light; they are beautiful, happy and both work perfectly, thank you". Remember to imagine your eyes full of light while you are saying this statement. You could even add a lot more details about the eye. The eye is made up of different parts like the retina, lens, cornea, optic nerve and iris. You could combine all these into your statement. "My retina is full of light; my lens is full of light; my cornea is full of light, my optic nerve is full of light". After you have mentioned them all, then carry on with the rest of the statement. This will deepen the meditation and you will focus closely on any area of the body that needs extra help and healing. This can be done with all the different parts of the body. Break them down and mention all the parts that make up that body part. Once you are happy with your chosen body parts and you have gone through the meditation routine, then, at the end, say, "I feel great". Keep this feeling close to you and try to hold onto it throughout the day.

You can have a go at both meditation exercises for yourself as I have shown but also for any family member, friend or neighbour who you think needs some help with their body, or even if they are struggling with an aspect of their life and need some support. All you need to do is imagine them in the light and not you. Then, say the same statements using their name.

All three of these meditations that I have shown you can be used throughout the day, anywhere you are and even when you are busy. If you are having a bad day and feeling down, angry or upset, do either one of the light exercises or blank your mind if you haven't got much time free – I would suggest the meditation to blank your mind. This can be done in any situation and will help to dissolve away any negative feelings. You can then be calm amid any chaos – have a go and try it. The more you meditate, the easier things will get. You will feel more in control, calmer and more centred.

You quiet the mind to find the peace within, then the peace is easier to find. Then, you may start to feel at peace a little more and then even more, the more you meditate.

Please have a go; you have so much to gain by meditating and keeping up the practice – see for yourself, relax and enjoy.

REVIEW

Let us go over what has been written in Chapter Nine – To Help You – Part Two.

Be Out in Nature
Nature will soothe you both inside and outside with its beauty. Appreciate all you see and feel; embrace the outdoors.

Find Yourself in Everyone You Meet
See yourself in everyone you meet every single day and then you will get on much better.

Looking Inwards to Find Peace
Peace will steady you in life. Find that peace so that you can always carry it within you.

Meditation
Meditation is so important – have a go and give it your all; keep up the regular routines every day or every other day. Notice what it will bring forth.

FOCUSING ON CHAPTER NINE – TO HELP YOU – PART TWO

STATEMENTS TO SAY OUT LOUD:

- *I will appreciate all the beauty around me.*
- *I will stop and admire nature.*
- *I will see myself in others.*
- *I will be mindful of other people's feelings.*
- *I will feel and find peace.*
- *I will sit quietly and listen to the silence.*
- *I will encourage peace to fill every part of my body until I am relaxed. I will hold onto that peace inside and then carry it around all day. I will then start again each morning.*
- *I am peace.*
- *I will practise meditation every day.*
- *Meditation will bring positive change to my life.*

I am love.

TEN

HELPING OTHERS TO HELP YOURSELF

TREAT EVERYONE HOW YOU WANT TO BE TREATED

It is so easy to moan about a neighbour or the man you bumped into at Tesco, the person who cut across you while driving. Have you ever wondered how their day is going? It is not just about you; it is also about all of us. Together, equal, alive, now in this moment. Sharing the space that you live in at that moment in time. So, in that moment, are you going to make someone happy or sad, confused or embarrassed, angry, depressed or content? You have all that power to make a big difference in someone's life. Now, you may think this is a little thing, but in fact, it is an enormous thing. Now think, you will make that person you encounter feel one of many emotions which will affect them so much that it will have a knock-on effect. They will then take out their frustration, anger, depression on the next person that they meet up with. Then, not only that person but the next person they encounter will also carry that on to who they meet. Then, they will do the same to who they encounter (do you see my point?). What a big difference the way you are can have on so many lives without you knowing or realising. So many, ten, fifteen, twenty or even more people could be affected. Let us hope that next time you go out your front door you will affect all those people with positive emotion: happiness, peace and laughter.

One of the most important sayings I have heard is: "treat everyone how you would like to be treated". This statement is so important and so true. If you look closely at this saying, it is profound. If everyone carried out this saying all over the world, no one would ever kill or even dare to hurt anyone as they would not want that to happen to them. What a difference this would make to the world. Everyone treating each other with respect, care, kindness and thoughtfulness. That then leads to being true and honest. The list could go on and on.

A lot of people say, "mind over matter". It is important to have a positive attitude as much as you possibly can, including faith, hope and intention for good. You see, the more negative you are, it will affect your body, mind and soul. You will get stuck in a rut. A positive attitude and thinking will help to have that knock-on effect that everyone will feel. People will then start to make you feel better. I noticed myself that the more positive I was in my everyday activities – maybe I was paying a bill, getting a food shop or just browsing – the more strangers I met started to say "take care" or "have a nice day". This happened two or three times a day, whenever I went into different shops. I found this unusual as for years before, everyone just said thank you and bye. So, of course, when these different people said, "take care", especially strangers, I took notice. I came to realise that it was just my positive attitude and my politeness when I said please and thank you or "have a nice day". My eye contact and smile were also important. What a difference these tiny actions make and the positivity you get back from the people who you give it to. If you are moody, miserable or not friendly, then no one will want to talk to you, look at you or go near you. The vibes you give out will affect everyone. I would like you to try this the next time you go out. Here are a few ideas:

1. All day, smile at strangers you pass or meet. You will find them doing the same back to you.
2. Share a word or two with someone near you or when you're in a shop. You will notice people talking back to you.
3. Say please and thank you and make eye contact. You will start to feel that positive energy building up even higher.

When you arrive home, please try not to lose that positive outlook. Use everything I have mentioned for your home life too. Let your family members see your positive energy; they may ask you about the change they see in you. Then, you can explain to them what you have been doing while out and about. Hopefully, they will follow your lead and start to do the same. They are such an easy couple of things to do. This will then make a calm, happy family unit to be a part of. All you must do is remember to treat everyone in your life or who you meet the way you would like to be treated. With kindness, gentleness, calmness and patience, interest, care, love, compliments, sensitivity, encouragement and always with a big smile.

PASSING ON YOUR KNOWLEDGE AND WISDOM

Always feel proud of what you have accomplished in life as you get older and mature. You may have had a very interesting job. You may have met a lot of different and interesting people on your journey so far. Maybe you are good at a certain skill, or you may know a lot about a certain subject. You could be a wonderful cook or fix anything around the house that goes wrong. When you notice younger people around you, start to pass on all these different things for them to learn about. You can also pass on your knowledge to friends, family and even strangers that you meet. You could make a big difference helping someone in ways you will never know. You will also feel proud and happy to know that you have helped one person or even hundreds of people. See how you can make that difference with the knowledge and skills that you have.

If you have learnt something from a sad situation in your life, please think about helping other people who are struggling in the same situation. Express your feelings and talk about what you have been through. You could pass on this information through the internet. Maybe you could do a YouTube video, or you could design and print out leaflets/posters to hand out. You may like to write a letter or send an email. You could ring round until you find the correct people who can also help you, like placing an advert in your local paper.

If you have any information that could help to make someone's life better, then please find the right people that need it and pass it on to them. Give back whenever you can and *make the world a better place.*

COMPLIMENT EVERYONE YOU MEET

I heard someone the other day say, "I always compliment people that I meet". When I heard this, I realised that this is a wonderful thing to do. I have sometimes complimented my friends but mainly my family. I'll say something like, "you look nice in that top" or "I love your bag". I really love the idea of complimenting every single person you meet, all day long and every day. Of course, if that someone is angry it probably will not work. I would suggest complimenting everyone apart from those people who are angry or you can tell would not appreciate it. The people you compliment will be so happy, and it is such an easy and simple thing to do. What better way to make someone feel good about themselves? You could be the one person who will help them to have a great day, just from giving a simple compliment. It may seem such a little thing to do, but small actions really can make a huge difference to someone's life. I am going to start complimenting everyone I talk to, from this moment on. I hope you will do it with me too.

My first compliment will be to you: I think you will be amazing at complimenting all the new people you meet throughout the day and following week.

Here are some more compliments you could use:

"You have a lovely, fantastic, wonderful, great, one of a kind, beautiful, or simply say I like your, hat, top, dress, boots, hairstyle, hair colour, glasses, make-up, tattoo, beard, teeth, watch, ring, nails, earrings, car, bike, pet, bag, smile, or I like what you have done with that/how that outfit looks so great on you, your design, your idea, your style, or you are a fantastic friend/mum".

The list could go on and on. I am sure you will notice other new compliments to give to each new person you bump into. Also, make sure that it is an appropriate time to compliment them. Sometimes you will have to leave it and wait for someone else instead.

Compliments will make everyone feel happy, including you because you are giving the compliment.

UNDERSTANDING AND AWARENESS

Please, look around you at what is going on in front of your face, body and in the space around you. Sometimes we really live in our own world and carry on like robots, or we just keep our heads down, maybe on our phone. Do not forget what it is to be alive. Be aware of all that is around you and taking place; be understanding and open when talking to someone.

If someone starts to talk negatively about a person, don't join in the conversation. That person isn't even there to defend themselves; change the subject or say, "I really like that person you are talking about; don't say that about them". That hopefully will stop them in their tracks. If it doesn't, then just walk away and never be a part of any negative comments. Put yourself in other people's shoes. This will give you a new perspective on what they are feeling and going through. This way, you can also let things go that normally would have upset you.

It is about understanding that life can be difficult. Everyone has hard days; everyone can feel down and upset. It is understanding that sometimes we need a helping hand or someone to listen to. It is also being tolerant and knowing that if someone is having a bad day, it will pass, and this moment won't last long. Understand the situation that presents itself and know that it will fade away.

Understanding can also be used to benefit all situations and all emotions, from sad and depressed to angry and frustrated. If you can look at all the scenes in front of you using understanding, it will be a lot easier to deal with. Be aware that it is not just you and everyone has to cope the best way they can; we can all sometimes suffer in some way. Understanding is so important in these delicate situations that occur in people's lives. Please think about how you can be more understanding in your own life and with all the different people you meet, including family, friends, neighbours and work colleagues. *Use understanding and be understanding.*

HERO

Heroes are people who make a difference in someone's life. It could be a simple thing which will mean the world to the person or a big thing like stepping forward at the right time to help someone in distress or to save someone's life. Being a hero in everyday life is all about making the effort to help someone in some small way.

If you help someone, you will become a hero. Be bold; be brave; be decisive; and stand up straight. Do the right thing; you may stand out or you may feel uncomfortable. The main thing is that you are doing good. Always choose right from wrong. If you notice someone being bullied and you stand there and watch it all without getting help or stepping forward, you will then become part of that moment in time. You will allow the bullying to take place. The memory will stay with you, without you even realising it. You must try to make a difference, even in a small way.

You could visit someone who is lonely, leave some food out for the birds or not kill any ants, bees, flies or spiders; instead, put an old see-through glass over the spider or fly and then find a thin piece of card, for example an old Christmas card, and slide it under the glass so that the spider or fly is still inside, and then carry the glass outside and find somewhere to let the spider, fly, bee or bug go free. Do not kill anything living. Before I leave this subject, I would like to mention that if you ever by chance find a fly floating in your bath or sink, scoop it out on a piece of kitchen towel and leave it on the bathroom shelf or somewhere safe out of the way. When the fly dries, it will sometimes still be alive and will fly away, and sometimes it won't. I know because I have done exactly this a few times. The main thing is that you tried to save it and didn't just flush it down the drain. Maybe then you will become a flies, spiders, bees or bugs hero.

Now, getting back to where I left off from. You could become a child's hero by playing with them or you could pass on your books to someone who loves to read. Any tinned food that you have spare, give to the food bank. There are so many positive things you can do to help the people in your community or even strangers that you meet.

Heroes are people doing little things in everyday life to help other people, selflessly, with no benefits to themselves. Making a difference in other people's lives is such a wonderful thing to do. You really will make the world a better place by becoming one of the many heroes.

Look after the helpless and weak. Look after the young and old; stand proud and tall doing the right thing. Be and set the example to all so that everyone can see the benefits of helping others. Stand out with goodness, choose right and then be right. Remember that by helping people, you will become that hero; shine your light for the good of all – *be a hero.*

REVIEW

Let us go over what has been written in Chapter Ten – Helping Others to Help Yourself.

Treat Everyone How You Want to Be Treated
This is so important in life. Always treat everyone how you want to be treated, with kindness, care, support and love.

Passing on Your Knowledge and Wisdom
Feel fantastic and proud to have so much to give to people. Your experience, your wisdom, your knowledge, advice and wonderful ideas.

Compliment Everyone You Meet
Bring a smile to everyone's face by complimenting them. This will also bring you joy to see their reaction.

Understanding and Awareness
Be aware of what is going on around you. Understand and be understanding towards everyone. We are all trying our best in this life. Be aware of everything going on around you; help to make the journey of life easier with your understanding.

Hero
Be that hero for everyone you meet, even strangers. The difference you will make in people's lives will really help to make the world a better place.

FOCUSING ON CHAPTER TEN – HELPING OTHERS TO HELP YOURSELF

STATEMENTS TO SAY OUT LOUD:

- *I will treat everyone how I want to be treated.*
- *I am full of joy.*
- *I will respect everyone who I meet.*
- *I will be thoughtful in my action and words towards others.*
- *I will smile at everyone that I meet.*
- *I will pass on what I have learnt to help others.*
- *I will try to make the world a better place. Giving my help, encouragement, patience, care and love to all.*
- *I will compliment myself every day.*
- *I will compliment everyone I meet.*
- *I will learn to be understanding in all situations.*
- *I will be aware of all around me.*
- *I will be a hero for someone today.*
- *I will not hurt any living thing.*
- *I will help as many people as I can.*
- *I will be brave.*
- *I am a brave person.*
- *I choose the positive path in life, using love as my guide.*
- *Love is the answer, so I will love.*

I am love.

ELEVEN

BE THE BEST YOU CAN BE

SHOW THE BEST OF YOU

What can I say but be the best you can be in all situations that arise? Life is for the living, and that means giving it your best shot and trying the best that you can, even if you are finding everything too much. You may need to refocus in a different direction so that you can move forward positively, completely focused on what needs to be done. Maybe you could change jobs, change location, interests or hobbies.

Change everything until it feels just right for you and you have that enthusiasm to give it your one hundred per cent commitment. When you feel that, then you will know you are on the right path for you. It is great when you feel motivated;

this will give you loads of extra ideas and enthusiasm to deal with difficult issues that come up around you in everyday living. Enjoy your life by making the right decisions for you. Once you are content, look for new developments that will start to appear in your life, giving you new opportunities to develop onwards and upwards. Also, by showing everyone around you the best of who you can be, you will encourage them to also try that bit harder.

Positivity in any situation will give encouragement to all, as it can be contagious and we all like to be around positive, happy, enthusiastic people. Remember that it is all about being the best you can in all that you do. Appreciate what and who is around you; acknowledge all the help you receive; embrace your family, friends, colleagues or acquaintances. Encourage them with your positive outlook and show them how life is meant to be lived, with joy, enthusiasm and hard work.

ENJOY YOUR FIVE DIFFERENT SENSES

We have five main senses that we use: taste, touch, sight, smell and sound. We are so lucky and should be so thankful that we have all these senses to enjoy throughout life, to experience everything to its fullest. Unfortunately, some people don't get to use all their senses and miss out, so please think about how you can enjoy using your body to its full potential through the senses that you have. Let us take a closer look at each of the five senses.

Taste:

We are so lucky to be able to taste the different foods from around the world. Everyone has so much variety and abundance of foods. We all have our favourites – I like roast dinner or salmon and broccoli. It is wonderful to experience all these foods that taste so different. Meals are so comforting and are very important for our health. Being able to taste everything is a wonderful gift which we should all appreciate and enjoy. Find some new recipes and have a go at making some new, delicious meals for yourself, friends and family. Enjoy all the different flavours.

Touch:

Touch is so important, and we take this so much for granted. Think of all the different situations we use touch in. To hold our loved ones and comfort each other. To feel what is around us in everyday life. From making food to washing ourselves and everyday activities that we all use touch for. We need to feel if things are safe or unsafe; the number of times we use our hands to touch every day is constant. To be able to feel different textures is so interesting and makes life exciting. Here are some examples: bumpy, smooth, soft, wet, cold, hot, fluffy, rough, sharp, bouncy, crinkly, bendy, hairy, grooved, bubbly, hard, silky, prickly, velvety.

We use touch to show our love to each other. It is such an amazing thing to be able to touch – please remember this and enjoy using touch.

Sound:

We get to hear all the wonderful sounds in life: birds singing, music, pets, doorbell, films, rain, wind, laughter. Hearing what your loved ones say and understanding what is being said out loud, quickly and easily. How lucky we are to hear what is going on around us. I bet we all take it for granted and don't think about what effect being able to hear has on our lives. Please realise this and enjoy hearing the wonderful sounds of life.

Smell:

It is great to be able to smell some fantastic things in our lives, like grass, flowers, perfume and food. We can also smell some unpleasant things, like if your baby needs a nappy change, food that has gone off or food that we don't like. We can smell things that are dangerous like smoke from a fire, gas and toxic fumes. We use smell in our lives every day and don't even think about it. So, I want you to think about it now. Realise how wonderful it is to smell all the different fragrances and aromas in your life and how different it would be if we couldn't use this sense. Be aware of all the different smells in your life.

Sight:

This sense is such a massive part of our lives. That is to be able to see. This enables us to have such a wide, complex and detailed awareness of everything in our life as vision shows us what, who and where we are.

You can see who is near you. You can also see who is happy or sad, what is going on around you minute by minute, what you look like. You can then choose what clothes you would like to wear. You can see where you live and what style of furniture and decorations you like. You can see where you're going when you walk around the house, go out to work, go shopping, to visit a friend or on holiday. You can also drive a car, ride a bike or do several sports, like running. You can see danger and help anyone you see. Also, you can see the beauty of life and the magical moments we all take for granted.

The happiness, love and laughter are all things we see in life and then look back on as happy memories and cherish all that we looked upon. Sight is used constantly and during every part of the day until it is time to go to sleep. We do not all realise this and probably take it for granted. Please remember how important and precious sight is in your life. Be thankful and really enjoy and cherish seeing the beauty around you. Make lots of happy memories in your life.

Now, *open your eyes* and really see the beauty all around you.

REMEMBER YOU'RE BEAUTIFUL

Beautiful outside:
There is so much pressure from advertisements, TV, films, books, your phone and everywhere you look on how you should present yourself and how you should look. Also, every season a new fashion statement and trends on what to wear are shown around the world. Please don't let this worry or upset you. Everyone is different; everyone has different taste in clothes and different ideas on how to look.

The main thing is that no one is completely perfect; this being the case, we are perfect in our imperfections. Everyone has different things about them that they are happy about, maybe small, dainty feet, long eyelashes, soft hair or a smooth complexion. We all have something that we like about ourselves. We also may have other attributes that we don't notice but other people admire about us. We really need to focus on these positive things about ourselves and not focus on the areas that we are unhappy about. If not, we will become so focused just on the negatives, which probably are not at all what you think. Everyone else, if you asked them or explained what you don't like about yourself, would say, "what are you talking about?" or "you're perfectly fine – I don't notice anything different about you". Sometimes we just see things a lot more negatively than they are, including how we look. We seem to exaggerate things in our mind, when in fact, everything is perfectly fine.

Show off all the things you like about yourself and stop brooding on what only you imagine are the negative bits. Please, realise that any negative thoughts are a waste of your energy and will only make you tired and miserable for no reason. Also, please don't worry or focus too much on the latest fashion or what you believe you should wear. Instead, just wear whatever makes you feel nice, comfortable and happy.

Beauty within:
Remember that you are not just beautiful outside, but you're also beautiful inside. Show off all that beauty within you with good action and good/positive communication towards everyone who you meet and towards all your family and friends.

Beauty is being caring, loving, kind, encouraging, enthusiastic, happy, peaceful, comforting, sympathetic, understanding, and I'm sure there are many more attributes you can think of. Show off all that beauty you possess to help make your life and others' around you amazing.

The more beauty you show everyone, the more beauty you will find on your journey ahead.

LAUGHTER AND JOY

Life should be full of laughter and joy. So, enjoy life and try not to be too hard on yourself. Lift yourself up with the lightness and fullness of joy. Watch a new comedy or watch something that you know makes you laugh at least once a week. Watch a stand-up comedian on YouTube, buy a DVD or watch something on the television. Read a book that makes you smile; do whatever brings you joy, laughter and happiness. If you know that someone will bring a smile to your face, then add speaking to them as part of your regular routine in life.

You want to lift your heart with the joy and laughter that comes from life. If you don't feel that anything makes you laugh or brings out your happiness, then please start today by finding out what will bring out the smile and laughter in you. It will then bubble up inside and you will notice how everyone wants to be around you because you will be beaming with joy.

Remember to live with that joy in your life.

LIFE IS AN ADVENTURE

Life really is an adventure; you get to choose to do whatever you want. Everything is about free will and choosing from moment to moment how you want to live. This is wonderful if you think about it – you are most definitely in your own adventure. You get to make it as exciting as you want it to be.

There are so many paths to choose from in life. Which job will you choose? Will you decide to have lots of hobbies or travel around the world? Will you have children or decide to buy a pet? The choice is yours only. I would say enjoying life to the fullest with all its opportunities is what we must all do in a safe, sensible way for ourselves and everyone involved.

You can experience the wonders of this life with its bending paths, rough climbs and sometimes abrupt halts or sticking points, but also the smooth and beautiful sights and experiences along the way. Life is amazing and we should cherish every step of the adventure. Helping each other along the way so that, together, we have a life full to the brim with experiences.

Now, let us look at another adventure; let us be aware of our life adventure and realise how wonderful that can be. Choose light, love, peace, fun and happiness along the way.

Make your life the best adventure it can be.

REVIEW

Let us go over what has been written in Chapter Eleven – Be the Best You Can Be.

Show the Best of You
Enjoy life and be the best you can in all situations presented to you. Commitment, enthusiasm and hard work will bring you amazing results and you will feel proud and so happy being you.

Enjoy Your Five Different Senses
Appreciate all the different senses that you use every day. Smell, taste, touch, sight and sound. We can use these to experience life to its fullest. So, use each one to experience life and all its wonders.

Remember You're Beautiful
Always remember you are beautiful inside and out. Shine that beauty for all to see. Show everyone how beauty is always there in every movement and action you take and every word you speak. Stand tall and proud of how beautiful you are.

Laughter and Joy
Add into your life that laughter and joy so that it overflows onto everyone you meet day to day. Be happy and feel how light and full of enthusiasm for life you start to be.

Life Is an Adventure
Life is a wonderful adventure. Choose and make decisions in your life that will give you joy, happiness, laughter, peace and love along the way.

FOCUSING ON CHAPTER ELEVEN – BE THE BEST YOU CAN BE

STATEMENTS TO SAY OUT LOUD:

- *I am motivated to try my best in all situations presented in life.*
- *I will be the best that I can be.*
- *I will work hard and try my best.*
- *I will enjoy using all my senses to the full.*
- *I will appreciate and acknowledge using my sense of taste.*
- *I will appreciate and acknowledge using my sense of touch.*
- *I will appreciate and acknowledge using my sense of sound.*
- *I will appreciate and acknowledge using my sense of smell.*
- *I will appreciate and acknowledge using my sense of sight.*
- *I am so lucky to use my senses.*
- *I am beautiful.*
- *I am beautiful outside and inside.*
- *I will shine my beauty for all to see.*
- *I love being beautiful.*
- *I will laugh every day.*
- *I will try to make everyone I meet smile or laugh.*
- *I will smile at everyone I meet throughout the day.*
- *I am full of joy, happiness and laughter.*
- *My life is the best adventure.*
- *I will choose all things to make my life's adventure happy, peaceful, full of joy, laughter and love.*
- *I am happy in my life's adventure.*
- *I choose to have an adventure.*

I am love.

STATEMENTS TO HELP YOU

I have written out some sayings – these are things that you can do. Please tick them off, one by one, until you have finished doing them all; then you can start again and again. Either copy them out or make a new list and print it out.

SAYINGS CHECKLIST:

☐ Be strong
☐ Be firm
☐ Be true
☐ Be kind
☐ Be gentle
☐ Be caring
☐ Be giving
☐ Be fun
☐ Be encouraging
☐ Be positive
☐ Be helpful
☐ Be good
☐ Be sensitive
☐ Be doing
☐ Be creative
☐ Be confident
☐ Be happy

☐ Be loving
☐ Be peaceful
☐ Be patient
☐ Be content
☐ Be childlike
☐ Be innocent
☐ Be brave
☐ Be free
☐ Be understanding
☐ Be calm
☐ Be responsible
☐ Be thoughtful
☐ Be healthy
☐ Be proud
☐ Be successful
☐ Be considerate
☐ Be mindful

- [ ] Be joyful
- [ ] Be tactful
- [ ] Be welcoming
- [ ] Be sharing
- [ ] Be committed
- [ ] Be fulfilled
- [ ] Be energised
- [ ] Be accepting
- [ ] Be still
- [ ] Be sympathetic
- [ ] Be eager
- [ ] Be honest
- [ ] Be individual
- [ ] Be unafraid
- [ ] Be vibrant
- [ ] Be forgiving
- [ ] Be present
- [ ] Be thankful
- [ ] Be a teacher
- [ ] Be open-minded
- [ ] Be open to change
- [ ] Be selfless
- [ ] Stop anything negative
- [ ] Say sorry
- [ ] Give a compliment
- [ ] Say I love you
- [ ] Ask for help

- [ ] Ask for advice
- [ ] Pass on your knowledge
- [ ] Learn something new
- [ ] Give someone advice
- [ ] Make someone smile
- [ ] Make a new friend
- [ ] Inspire someone
- [ ] Hold someone's hand
- [ ] Change a negative into a positive
- [ ] Fix something for someone
- [ ] Play a game
- [ ] Have a day trip
- [ ] Let it go
- [ ] Stop worrying
- [ ] Buy a gift for someone
- [ ] Sing
- [ ] Dance
- [ ] Believe
- [ ] Have faith
- [ ] Joke
- [ ] Laugh
- [ ] Heal
- [ ] Exercise
- [ ] Hug

POSITIVE WORDS

Here is a list of some positive words for you to focus on, or you could use them to inspire you.

Able	Abundant
Accept	Acceptance
Accommodate	Accomplishment
Admirable	Adorable
Adventurous	Affection
Amazed	Amazing
Angel	Angelic
Astounding	Awakening
Awesome	Beaming
Beautiful	Beauty
Best	Bliss
Blissful	Blooming
Bold	Bountiful
Brave	Bright
Brightness	Brilliant
Bubbly	Captivating
Carefree	Caring
Charming	Colourful
Complete	Content
Continue	Creativity

Cuddly

Cute

Dance

Dazzling

Dear

Definitely

Delicious

Delightful

Divine

Doing

Eager

Earnest

Easy-going

Ecstasy

Ecstatic

Elegant

Embrace

Enchanting

Encouragement

Energetic

Energised

Enjoyment

Enlightened

Enthralling

Enthusiasm

Excellent

Exceptional

Expressive

Exquisite

Fabulous

Fair

Faithful

Family

Fantastic

Fascinating

Fine

Fluffy

Forgiveness

Free

Fresh

Friendship

Fulfilled

Fun

Generous

Gentle

Gift

Gifted

Giving

Glittering

God

Golden

Good

Gorgeous

Graceful

Grand

Gratitude

Greatness

Growing

Happy

Healed

Healthy	Heart
Heart-warming	Helpful
Heroic	Holy
Homelike	Honest
Honour	Honourable
Honoured	Hope
Humane	Humble
Ideal	Ideas
Individual	Innocence
Insightful	Interesting
Inventions	Inviting
Join	Jolly
Jovial	Joy
Joyful	Just
Kindly	Kindness
Kinglike	Kiss
Kissable	Knowing
Knowledge	Laughter
Light	Lightness
Like	Lovable
Love	Lovely
Loving	Loyalty
Lush	Luxurious
Magnificent	Majestic
Marvellous	Merriment
Mesmeric	Mighty
Mindful	Miracle
Nestled	New
Nice	Nifty
Nurture	OK

Omnipresent	Oneness
Open-minded	Optimistic
Outstanding	Overflowing
Painless	Pamper
Passionate	Patience
Peaceful	Perfect
Persevere	Playful
Pleasing	Positive
Pretty	Proud
Pure	Quaint
Quality	Quiet
Radiance	Radiant
Ready	Refined
Restful	Rewarding
Right	Robust
Rosy	Satisfied
Saved	Sharing
Shimmering	Shining
Significant	Sing
Skilful	Smile
Soft	Soulfulness
Sparkling	Special
Spectacular	Splendid
Steadfast	Steady
Stillness	Strength
Strong	Stunning
Sublime	Successful
Super	Superb
Sweetness	Sympathetic
Tactful	Talent

Tasteful	Teachable
Teacher	Tender
Tender-Hearted	Terrific
Thankfulness	Timeless
Thoughtful	Toasty
Thoughtfulness	Tranquil
Thrilled	True
Thriving	Uber
Timely	Unaffected
Top-notch	Understanding
Triumphant	Valiant
Truth	Venturous
Ultra	Vibrant
Unafraid	Warm
Unique	Welcoming
Venture	Whole
Versatile	Wonderful
Wacky	Xenial
Warmed	X Factor
Whimsical	Yes
Winning	Yippee
Wow	Zeal
Xenium	Zing
XO	Zappy
Yay	Zest

THINGS YOU COULD DO – INSIDE AND OUTSIDE

INSIDE – THINGS TO DO:

Read

Draw

Paint

Make something

Colouring book

Modelling

Sculpture

Dot-to-dot

Splatter painting

Thumbprint painting

Design something

Cake decorating

Handprint

Potato stamps

String art

Scrapbooking

Play charades

Play Twister

Make cards

Sing

Watch something

Collage

Sew

Knit

Stained glass

Play dough

Origami

Sock puppets

Jigsaw

Crossword

Card games

Computer games

Board games

Party games

Make bookmarkers

Cooking

Indoor camping

Indoor treasure hunt

Play an instrument

Model crafting

Dance
Lego
Perform karaoke
Start a collection
Start a journal
Make lemonade
Meditate
Cardboard playhouse
Jewellery making
Darts
Do a spa evening
Play "I spy"
Do a sports evening
Have date nights
Create a cocktail
Memory jar
Pillow fight
Make your own board game
Collect and paint rocks
Make paper snowflakes
Cardboard tube marble run
Create a family recipe book
Have a fashion show
Have a tea party
Learn magic tricks
Make a comic strip
Write some poetry
Set up a murder mystery
Make friendship bracelets
Make a blanket fort

Play hide-and-seek
Learn some sign language
Make a sun-catcher
Research your family tree
Interview family members
Look at family albums
Have a treat day
Have a staring contest
Make a photo booth
Make a time capsule
Learn a foreign language
Practise yoga
Science day
Photography
Do chores
Have themed dinners
Pottery
Stand-up comedy
Calligraphy
Floristry
Animal shadows
Chess
Produce electronic music
Family game night
Beanbag toss
Play dress up
Make paper chains
Make paper planes/flowers
Make a jewellery box
Make a man cave

Make a den for the children
Throw a birthday party
Try a new food
Make a rag doll
Make a car racing track
Make music using bottles
Draw yourself or family members
Write a short story and then tell it
Rearrange furniture and nick-nacks
Have a clear out around the house
Make puppets and put on a show
Make a cardboard doll's house/buildings/people
Create your own film or music festival
Have a day planning trips and things to do outside
Make gift baskets for family, friends and neighbours
Find space to make your own walk-in wardrobe
Create a vision board of things you want to achieve and
    your dreams for the future

OUTSIDE – THINGS TO DO:

Birdwatching	Feed the ducks
Blow bubbles	Have a treasure hunt
Rounders	Play minigolf
Football	Badminton
Catch	Hopscotch
Walk the dog	Collect seashells
Nature walk	Make a bird feeder
Skipping	Make a shed
Bowling	Gardening
Tennis	Have a slip and slide
Go fishing	Build a tree house
Jump on a trampoline	Play swing ball
Build a sandcastle	Camping
Skim stones across the sea	Go hiking
Press flowers	Barbecue
Use binoculars	Fireworks
Sing songs	Build a fort
Make daisy chains	Wash the car
Play dodgeball	Have a race
Play catch	Egg and spoon race
Ride a bike	Frisbee
Walk/jog	Play hide-and-seek
Water gun fight	Make a scarecrow
Look for bugs	Fly a drone
Build a den	Fly a kite
Stargazing	Hunt for worms
Plant a garden	Splash in puddles
Have a picnic	Build a snowman

Snowball fight
Go sledging
Watch the sunset/sunrise
Grow a herb garden
Sleep under the stars
Relax in a hammock
Play table tennis
Have a campfire
Torch tag
Have a car boot sale
Juggle
Whittling and carving
Restore a car/motorbike
Message in a bottle
Landscaping
Speed walking
Litter picking
Upcycling
Have a water fight
Look through a telescope
Collect rain in pots/pans
Raise money for someone
Create a fairy garden/house
Float boats down a stream
Catch raindrops on your tongue
Draw your home/nature around you
Chalk/water painting on pavement
Watch clouds and pick out different pictures
Relax and have fun in an inflatable pool

A LIST OF DIFFERENT PLACES TO VISIT AND WHAT YOU COULD EXPERIENCE

.

A road trip
Aquarium
Arcade
Botanical garden
Nature centre/reserve
Festival
Farm
Outdoor concert
Waterpark
Sporting baths
Zoo
Galleries
Beach
Visit national monuments
Visit a historical site
Go wine tasting
Ride a hot-air balloon
Paddle a canoe
Skiing/snowboarding
Visit a forest

Skydiving
Rowing
Roller skating
Hockey
Skateboarding and BMX
Ice skating
Boat trip
Learn to surf
Gymnastics
Cinema
Theatre
Ballroom
Hip-hop/breakdancing
Jazz
Tap dance
Irish dancing
Contemporary dance
Judo
Karate
Aikido

Kung Fu	Rugby
Boxing	Netball
Ride a motorbike	Athletics
Ride in a car	Driving
Zumba	Rock climbing
Brownies/Guides	Visit friends/family
Playground	Ballet
Restaurants	Wrestling
Cathedrals	Kickboxing
Amusement park	Taekwondo
Castles	Jiu-jitsu
Library	Mixed martial arts
Shops	Marathon
Museums	Volleyball
Swimming baths	Basketball
Church	Weightlifting
Wildlife areas	Parachuting
Visit statues	Parasailing
Horse riding	Diving with dolphins
Safari parks	Sailing
Lido park	Visit a hedge maze
Transport museum	Hiking
Karting	Hockey
Laser combat	Scouts/Cubs/Beavers
Bowling	Rambling
Soft-play	Snorkelling
Visit a waterfall	Metal detecting
Archery	Hang-gliding
Strawberry picking	Scuba-diving
Golf	Gold panning

Tai chi	Ghost hunting
Rock/mineral collecting	Geocaching
Trainspotting	Astronomy
Bungee jumping	Bingo
Lion dancing	Fencing
Belly dancing	

Be a tourist in your own city

Visit a railway station and have a steam day trip

There are many hobbies and activities to take part in to give you a happy and fulfilling life.

NAMES OF PLACES YOU COULD VISIT

England:

Wimbledon
Buckingham Palace
London Bridge
Big Ben
Covent Garden
Churchill War Rooms
London Eye
Natural History Museum
West End
Tower Of London
Camden Market
Little Venice
Eden Project
Minack Theatre
Land's End
St Michael's Mount
Newquay for surfing
Isles of Scilly
Malvern Hills
Cotswolds

The Lake District
Micheldever Wood
Brighton Royal Pavilion
Norfolk Lavender Centre
Stratford Town Walk
Wistman's Wood
Silverstone
Sherwood Forest
Westminster Abbey
Notting Hill
Hyde Park
Oxford Street
Palace of Westminster
Shakespeare's Globe Theatre
The National Gallery
The British Museum
Camel Valley Vineyard
Cheddar Gorge
Glastonbury Festival
Bath

Durdle Door

Kinver Rock Houses

Lulworth Cove

Clifton Suspension Bridge

Jurassic Coast

Hadrian's Wall

Stonehenge

Yorkshire Dales

Longleat Hedge Maze

Isle of Wight

Botanical Gardens

Peak District National Park

Cadbury World

Windsor Castle

Black Country Living Museum

Harry Potter Tour of Warner Bros

Birmingham Museum and Art Gallery

Scotland:

Inverness Castle

Scone Palace

North Coast 500

Glamis Castle

Ben Nevis

Edinburgh

The Jacobite Steam Train

Arthur's Seat

Glen Nevis Valley

Aberdeen Maritime Museum

Glen Coe Valley

Fort George

Urquhart Castle

Discovery Point

Loch Ness

Blair Athol Distillery

The Isle of Skye

Heads of Ayr Farm Park

The Isles of Lewis and Harris

Kelvingrove Art Gallery and Museum

Wales:

Snowdonia National Park

Beddgelert Forest

Three Cliffs Bay

Skomer Island

Conwy Castle

Château Rhianfa

Snowden

Tower, Mold

Silver Mountain Experience   Felinwynt Rainforest
Traeth Abermaw Beach   Whitmore Bay Beach
Caernarfon Castle   Tredegar House
Hafod Estate   Porthkerry Country Park
Vale of Rheidol Railway   Penrhyn Castle and Garden
Pembrey Country Park   Great Orme
Cilgerran Castle   National Slate Museum
Plas Cadnant Hidden Gardens
St Fagans National Museum of History

Northern Ireland:

Giant's Causeway   Dunluce Castle
The Dark Hedges   Carrickfergus Castle
Carrick-a-Rede Rope Bridge   Clare Glen Woodland
Glenoe Waterfall   Belfast City Hall
Tollymore Forest Park   Crumlin Road Gaol
Cushendun Village   Ballycastle Beach
Castle Coole   Marble Arch Caves
Enniskillen Castle   Rathlin Island
Titanic Belfast   The Derry Walls
Florence Court
Mount Stewart
Crawfordsburn Country Park
Cuilcagh Boardwalk Trail (Stairway to Heaven)

There are many more places to visit in Great Britain, from interesting towns and cities to beautiful countryside to go and experience.

FINAL WORD

One day, we are all – and I mean every single one of us – are going home. When it will happen, we don't know. This is a fact that we can't change the reality of. It is going to happen to me, you and everyone we know. So, if this is the case, we should really think about that fact. We will not be here one day. So, what would you like to have done to feel happy inside for when you leave here? I want to feel at peace when it is my time to leave. So, have a think about what you want to achieve or do before time speeds up and you are facing that moment in time, looking over your life. You of course will want to feel content with what you have done. Now would be a great time to start your memories. Build that picture up of what you want your family, friends and neighbours to know you for. Enjoy our lives, but at the same time, help people and become the best we can be. Find that peace within on our journey so that we find the hardships in life a lot easier to cope with. We also will be less stressed with everyday life – this will help us to grow in love, and then we will be able to give more love out to everyone around us.

I hope you enjoyed this book. Hopefully it will help you to view life with all the emotions we have in a slightly different way. Going forward, this will help you to live in a more positive manner. Please stay strong and find that peace within.

I wish you lots of happiness on your journey ahead.

Love to you all,

Sarah

X